Advance Praise for *Making the Connection*

"This book is by far the best thing I have read, apart from Scripture, on the pragmatic reality of God's desire to be in relationship with people. We can go to Google and instantly attain information, yet, nothing is as relevant as the truths laid out so simply in this book. Many times during the reading of this book I had to pause because I was awestruck at how much God loves us. In the context of these chapters, there is more packed, for one person to be able to digest in one life time. John Telman provides an exhilarating look at the beauty of our great God."

Edward Brost
International Corporate Businessman
(also working with Samaritans Purse and
the Billy Graham Evangelistic Association)

"One simply cannot read this book without sharing the contagious passion for our great God and Savior that John Telman describes so well. Our Lord is worthy! Join in His worship!"

Rev. Rick Wadholm, Jr.
Assistant Professor of Biblical and Theological Studies at
Trinity Bible College

"It was A.W. Tozer: who stated, "What comes into our minds when we think about God is the most important thing about us." In *Making The Connection: Discovering Who God Really Is* John Telman provides a thorough and inspirational engagement with the person and work of our God so that we can ponder and be transformed by who He is. A very worthwhile way to approach this book would be to read a chapter daily and then to prayerfully allow these truths to become real in ones heart and mind."

Dr. David R. Wells
General Superintendent of the
Pentecostal Assemblies of Canada

"...insightful...dynamic and a very practical book. It not only brings out John Telman's intimate relationship with Christ, but it also presents God Himself in all His glory. This treasure will inspire you to want to know Him and make Him known."

Terry L. Sleppy
Author of *The New American Standard Chronological Bible*

"I am happy to be able to recommend John Telman's book, *Making The Connection: Discovering Who God Really Is.* It is a superb presentation of many of the characteristics and nature of God; discussed in a direct, brief, understandable way that will help people know who God is, what He does for those who know Him, that He is desires an intimate relationship with each person, and how that relationship is possible through Jesus Christ."

Dr. George W. Westlake, Jr.
Pastor, Seminary Professor and
International Conference Speaker

EBook Versions of this book are available in
English, French, and Spanish.

FOREWORD BY ROBERT WHITE

MAKING THE
Connection

Discovering
WHO GOD
Really Is

JOHN W. TELMAN

MAKING THE CONNECTION
Copyright © 2014 by John W. Telman

All scripture quotations are taken from the NEW AMERICAN STANDARD BIBLE®, Copyright © 1960, 1962, 1963, 1968, 1971, 1972, 1973, 1975, 1977, 1995 by The Lockman Foundation. Used by permission.

Printed In Canada

ISBN: 978-1-4866-0488-3

Word Alive Press
131 Cordite Road, Winnipeg, MB R3W 1S1
www.wordalivepress.ca

Library and Archives Canada Cataloguing in Publication

Telman, John W., 1959-, author
    Making the connection : discovering who God really is / John W. Telman.

ISBN 978-1-4866-0488-3 (pbk.)

    1. God (Christianity). I. Title.

BT103.T45 2014   231   C2014-902288-3

To Carole

whom I admire, love, and treasure
as not only my wife but my friend.

Contents

Part Four: The Ministry of God

Acknowledgements

IT'S DIFFICULT TO NAIL DOWN ALL THE NAMES OF PEOPLE WHO contributed, in one way or another, resulting in this book. Beginning with Carole, Jeremy and the rest of the family, I've received more than enough encouragement to write. Then there have been many friends around the world who have had the right word at the right time to inspire me. In particular, I would like to thank Millie Gray who read through the original manuscript and gave constructive suggestions.

Mentors who have inspired me over the years include, Gordon Gabert, Hank Kalke, Dr. George Westlake Jr., Dr. Gus Konkel, Dr. Stanley Horton and my dear grandfathers, Jacobus Telman and John Harold Huckle.

I would also like to thank my dear friends, Dr. Dave. R Wells, Terry Sleppy, Rev. Rick Wadholm Jr., Edward Brost and Dr. George W. Westlake Jr., who read the original manuscript and have endorsed this book. Author and friend Robert White graciously has not only written the forward but has patiently guided me with my writing.

Without a doubt, I would be in error if I didn't give praise to my LORD and Savior Jesus Christ. With great patience and love, he has worked in my life and has shown me the glory of God.

—John Telman

Foreword

AT A RECENT SHIFTING STATS FORUM, SPONSORED BY WORLD VISION Canada and held at Tyndale Seminary, a participant tweeted a stat: eighty per cent of Canadians still believe in God. What wasn't explained in his one hundred and forty characters is whether or not that meant more than two-thirds of Canadians believe in the Judeo-Christian God as described and defined by the Bible. Perhaps it means there's an overwhelming belief in "god" in general, be it the God of the Bible, the God of the Torah, the god of the Koran, or any other multitude of deities which can be found among believers in Canada's multicultural, multi-faith culture.

I can tell you, based on a thirty-year career as a journalist who specialized in faith-based issues (including a decade as the editor of a regional Christian newspaper), that even those who believe in the God of the Bible often have an extremely skewed perspective of that God. And many of those on the fringes of Christianity have been wounded and alienated by those skewed perspectives. Some of us, rather than try to plumb those views with a true depiction of God found in the Bible, in John Telman's words, "tire of arguing [and] tend to hang out with those who hold the same beliefs" that we do.

Making the Connection: Discovering Who God Really Is attempts to put the corrective lens of scripture on the distorted view of God held by many. Telman writes like the pastor he is: with clarity, foresight, insight, and a longing to see people make the life-changing decision to follow God. Deftly weaving scripture with real-life examples, he creates a tapestry that depicts the whole of who God is: his character, his manifestations, his ministry, and most importantly, his importance in the life of a believer.

Telman's aim is best described in a chapter called "God is Light." Referring to the story of Job, he writes:

> *In Job 38–41, God answers [Job] with a description of who he is. God didn't defend himself by telling him that Satan had asked to test Job. Instead God shed light on who he is. It's so complete and overwhelming that Job said, "I have heard of You by the hearing of the ear, but now my eye sees You" (Job 42:5). The Hebrew word for sees is raah, which means that Job understood. He had an Aha! moment.*

It's from this aim that two different, but similar, audiences can find an Aha! moment in *Making the Connection*. The first audience is made of those on the fringes of Christianity, wounded by a skewed perspective, who really want to find out who God is. They want to know the truth about God and, in the end, find salvation through that search.

The other audience comprises Christians who have long struggled to find a way to explain who God is to family and friends. This handy reference to the nature and character of God provides the answers they've wanted to give.

And while Telman writes with a pastor's heart, and has the knowledge to plunge deep into the theology of who God is, he avoids theological language by writing equally for the person in the pew and on the street. May both find the Aha! moment of knowing who God is and making that vital, eternal connection with him.

—Robert White

Robert White is a freelance journalist from Guelph, Ontario who specializes in faith-based issues and served as the editor for ChristianWeek Ontario *from 2002 to 2012. His book* Chasing the Wind: Finding Meaningful Answers from Ancient Wisdom *was the winner of the non-fiction category of the 2010 Word Alive Press publishing contest.*

Introduction

A STUDENT ONCE TOLD HIS PROFESSOR, "I DON'T BELIEVE IN GOD." He was then asked to describe the God he didn't believe in.

"I probably don't believe in him, either," the wise teacher replied.

It is a sad fact that most people who don't believe in God have either an incomplete or false understanding of who the Almighty God is. This book, while valuable for such people, isn't intended to be an apologetic or a defense. Simply, between the covers of this book is one man's observations of the God who has made himself known.

Every person has distinct characteristics that are observable. God is no exception. When we introduce someone, we usually tell something about them after stating their name. In the case of God, we have three specific tools to help us describe who he is. First, we have creation, which presents a deity who is infinitely powerful. Secondly, we have scripture, which reveals God's desire to be known. Thirdly, we have our personal interactions with him. None of these tools contradict each other. In fact, they support each other so that an accurate understanding of who God is achieved.

One may wonder how the finite can know the infinite, but we must remember that it is God who has made himself known. If it was up to mankind, we would guess at who God is and we would be wrong; thankfully, knowing God is not up to us.

Jesus said, "He who has seen me has seen the Father" (John 14:9). He made it possible for us to know God in the flesh. Speaking of Jesus Christ, the apostle John wrote,

> *What was from the beginning, what we have heard, what we have seen with our eyes, what we have looked at and touched with our hands, concerning the Word of Life—and the life was manifested, and we have seen and testify and proclaim to you the eternal life, which was with the Father and was manifested to us—what we have seen and heard we proclaim to you also, so that you too may have fellowship with us; and indeed our fellowship is with the Father, and with His Son Jesus Christ.*
>
> I John 1:1–3

Along with Jesus Christ helping us to understand who God is, we have the added assistance of the Holy Spirit. The Holy Spirit was promised by Jesus (John 14:16–31) and continues to effectively reveal the truth of who God is.

We will resist discussing the Trinity, but it should be well-understood that all three—the Father, the Son, and the Holy Spirit—are active in mankind to bring an understanding of who God is.

There is so much that can be written about God, so much more than you will read in this book. Still, it is my hope that these observations magnify Almighty God and encourage the reader to draw close to the one who can be known. Each section will include short reflections that magnify realities concerning God.

Who Is This?

Everyone in this world has an opinion. Whether it's about a sports team, a restaurant dish, or even the weather, people have a point of view that invariably someone will disagree with. Since most tire of arguing, we tend to hang out with those who hold the same beliefs as us. It's sometimes fun to argue a point, but our minds struggle to stay calm with those who see things differently than we do. It's therefore not a common practice to hang out with those who have a difference of opinion.

A beautiful story is recorded in Luke 7. It's set at a meal in the house of a Pharisee named Simon. Jesus Christ was invited and accepted. Before looking at what happened, let's remind ourselves that Jesus and the Pharisees didn't see eye to eye. In fact, heated words were often exchanged. The Pharisees tested and plotted against Jesus (Matthew 12:14, 22:15) and Jesus scolded the Pharisees for their legalistic and uncaring practices (Matthew 23:13–33). On this occasion, it wasn't so much what was said but what was thought.

While Jesus and Simon were eating, a woman who was known to be a sinner by everyone expressed worship of Jesus in a most wonderful way. Without words, she cleaned the feet of Jesus with her tears, wiped them with her hair, and anointed his feet with expensive perfume.

Without words, Simon the Pharisee thought, *"If this man were a prophet He would know who and what sort of person this woman is who is touching Him, that she is a sinner"* (Luke 7:39). The fact is that Jesus knew who the woman was. Speaking to Simon, Jesus said, *"I say to you, her sins, which are many, have been forgiven, for she loved much"* (Luke 7:47).

Along with Simon, the others who were present began to say to themselves, *"Who is this man who even forgives sins?"* (Luke 7:49). In Luke 5:21 the Pharisees and scribes are said to have also reasoned, *"Who is this man who speaks blasphemies? Who can forgive sins, but God alone?"*

Who is Jesus Christ? There are many arguments concerning who Jesus is. Some deny that he is the Son of God. Some think he was "just" a good teacher, which is laughable since Jesus asserted over and over again that he is God.

What is most distinguishing about him is that he forgives. We'll look further at this God who forgives, but notably, in relation to humanity, God *actually* forgives. That may not mean much to some, but even the Pharisees acknowledged that only God could really pardon sin. That's precisely what Jesus did for the notorious woman in Luke 7. She expressed her extravagant worship because she was forgiven. No longer was she the one others looked down on. She was forgiven! She knew who Jesus Christ was. She didn't ask "Who is this?" because she was forgiven.

We know little about her, but we know much about Jesus Christ. Peter, a firsthand observer of what took place, long after said to the high priest and Sadducees,

The God of our fathers raised up Jesus, whom you had put to death by hanging Him on a cross. He is the one whom God exalted to His right hand as a Prince and a Savior, to grant repentance to Israel, and forgiveness of sins. And we are witnesses of these things.

Acts 5:30–32

Who is this one who billions worship? It is Jesus Christ the Son of God, the one who forgives. I know. He forgave me, and yet he is so much more!

The psalmist wrote, *"For the Lord is a great God and a great King above all gods, in whose hand are the depths of the earth..."* (Psalm 95:3–4). God is, and he may be known. He exists and is personal. These two facts are crucial to the life of every human being. He is the author of the world's bestseller, the Bible.

He is the healer of all diseases. (Isaiah 57:19, Isaiah 53:5)

He is the redeemer of mankind. (Titus 2:13–14)

He is creator of all that is. (Isaiah 40:28, Malachi 2:10)

He is the provider for all needs. (Philippians 4:19)

He comforts us. (2 Corinthians 1:3–4)

He gives us everything we need to live godly. (1 Peter 1:3)

He gives us power, love, and a sound mind. (2 Timothy 1:7)

He is the giver of eternal life. (1 John 5:11)

He gives us everything for our enjoyment. (1 Timothy 6:17)

HE IS WORKING IN US. (EPHESIANS 2:10)

HE IS THE LOVER OF ALL MANKIND. (1 JOHN 4:8, 16)

HE IS FAITHFUL. (2 THESSALONIANS 3:3)

HE IS SLOW IN ANGER AND GREAT IN POWER. (NAHUM 1:3)

HE IS IMPARTIAL. (ACTS 10:34)

HE IS STRONG. (REVELATION 18:8)

HE IS LIGHT. (1 JOHN 1:5, JOHN 12:46)

HE IS A CONSUMING FIRE. (HEBREWS 12:29)

HE IS OUR FATHER. (MALACHI 1:6)

HE IS ALMIGHTY. (GENESIS 17:1)

HE IS ALWAYS PRESENT. (MATTHEW 28:20)

HE IS HOLY. (1 PETER 1:16)

HE IS OUR FRIEND. (JOHN 15:14)

HE IS THE GOOD SHEPHERD. (JOHN 10:14, PSALM 23)

HE IS THE TRUTH AND THE LIFE. (JOHN 14:6)

HE IS SELF-SUFFICIENT. (JOHN 5:26)

These few facts are not exhaustive. They only scratch the surface about the truth of God. He is transcendent and unlimited by anything in this world or in the universe. Focusing on him naturally results in worship!

PART ONE:
The Character of God

God Forgives

WE COULD ARGUE ABOUT WHICH DEFINING CHARACTERISTIC OF GOD IS most profound. We would inevitably include the fact that God forgives. Without forgiveness, other characteristics would mean little. Oh how we are in need of forgiveness.

Jesus made a striking statement as he hung on a Roman cross. These three words still speak loudly throughout the centuries: *"Father, forgive them"* (Luke 23:34). Imagine. What kind of love is this that he would say such a thing while enduring the extreme pain of betrayal, abandonment, mockery, merciless beatings, and the torture of crucifixion?

When in pain, most of us don't consider others. We cry out for relief and sympathy. But listen to what Jesus said. He did not condemn. He did not spew hate or judgment. He spoke love.

In case anyone should think he was speaking strictly of the Roman soldiers, the truth is that he was speaking of all of us. The "them" is you and me! Jesus interceded on our behalf. Isaiah prophesied concerning the Messiah when he said that *"He Himself bore the sin of many, and interceded for the transgressors"* (Isaiah 53:12).

The strength of God the Father's ability to forgive is expressed in the sacrifice of the Son. That is the wonderful gospel.

God has actually extended forgiveness! And what a debt we owe him. Every time we tell God, by our choices, to mind his own business, we have sinned.

Even offences between people started out as sins against God. As offenders, we choose to ignore God, become selfish, self-protective, fearful, or angry, and then strike out against another. The disregard of God is sin against him. King David understood this when he repented of his murder of a man because of his own lust for a woman:

> *For I know my transgressions, and my sin is ever before me. Against You, You only, I have sinned and done what is evil in Your sight, so that You are justified when You speak and blameless when You judge.*
>
> Psalm 51:3–4

God would be righteous in judging a world that has largely ignored him, but the heart of the Father is revealed in Jesus' words to Nicodemus: *"For God did not send the Son into the world to judge the world, but that the world might be saved through Him"* (John 3:17).

Consider this story. A father and his daughter were walking through a grassy field. In the distance, they saw a prairie fire and realized that it would soon engulf them. The father knew there was only one way of escape. They quickly began a fire right where they were and burned a large patch of grass. When the huge fire drew near, they stood on the section that had already burned. The girl was terrified, but her father assured her, "The flames can't get to us. We are standing where the fire has already been."

Jesus was the perfect sacrifice for our sins, so when anyone stands where God's justice was satisfied—that is, in Christ—they are safe from the coming judgment. Let's respond to him in repentance because God forgives. Hallelujah!

God Hears

WHEN ROUGH TIMES COME, WE DESIRE TO BE HEARD. UNFORTUNATELY, friends and family may offer potential answers without really hearing us. Being heard is as much an answer to a problem as it is a plan. The beauty of God is reflected in his ability to hear us with his undivided attention.

God is all-knowing. Nothing is hidden from him. Every tiny detail about you and I is known by God. The psalmist said, *"You know it all"* (Psalm 139:4). And yet God doesn't act like a know-it-all. He doesn't offer solutions without hearing us completely. In fact, at times it may appear that God isn't acting on our behalf when, in reality, he understands that we initially need someone to listen to how we feel. I know this from experience.

From time to time, my son has told me about a problem he experienced. Too often I've made the mistake of proposing solutions before really hearing him out. Even though these solutions might work, he has seemed inconsolable. Perhaps what he really needed first was an ear to hear him. Oh I heard words, but missed how he was feeling.

Isn't God so wonderful? Not only does he have answers, he has a listening ear to hear our hearts' cry.

King David wrote a beautiful song that we find in 2 Samuel 22. He said, *"I will call upon the Lord, who is worthy to be praised"* (2 Samuel 22:4). He went on to say, *"In my distress I called upon the Lord, yes, I cried to my God; and from His temple He heard my voice, and my cry for help came into His ears"* (2 Samuel 22:7).

Imagine! God, the creator who sees and knows all, actually listens. He could speak, and he does, but first he listens. What wonderful grace and love he has for all of us.

Have you ever had a conversation with someone who's just waiting to speak? They are waiting for you to stop talking so they can offer their perspective. God, whose wisdom makes the total wisdom of man look ridiculous, isn't like that. He is patiently listening to each one who cries out to him. David knew this truth. It caused him to conclude, *"Therefore I will give thanks to You, O Lord, among the nations, and I will sing praises to Your name"* (2 Samuel 22:50).

In the midst of any and all issues of life, we can cry out to someone who listens to us and, like David, joyfully worship the God who hears us!

God Pardons

GOD SPOKE THROUGH THE PROPHET MICAH CONCERNING HOW horrendous sin is. Israel was a mess. Idolatry reigned. At the time of Micah, the creator wasn't worshipped; the god of self and the god of superstition was. This may not sound too serious to some, but idolatry caused Micah to mourn for his country. He said, *"I must lament and wail, I must go barefoot and naked"* (Micah 1:8). To go barefoot was to show others that he was mourning, and going without sandals was to go naked. It was a physical statement that something horrible had happened. Today, someone might wear a black armband to signify that they are mourning.

The first three chapters of Micah speak about the sin of Israel. The next two chapters contain a prophesy of the coming Messiah. The final two chapters tell of a conversation between God and Micah.

Micah closes with a wonderful comfort for humanity. He says, *"Who is a God like you, who pardons iniquity...?"* (Micah 8:18) God is the one who pardons (frees from punishment). He is the one who forgives us of the sin we have committed. No amount of good works could win our pardon.

Jesus healed the paralytic man and said to him, *"Son, your sins are forgiven"* (Mark 2:5). The scribes didn't like this. They said, *"Who can forgive sins but God alone?"* (Mark 2:7) Even they knew that only God is able to forgive sins.

God can deal with the sin issue with humanity, and he did!

> *For He [God] rescued us from the domain of darkness, and transferred us to the kingdom of His beloved Son, in whom we have redemption, the forgiveness of sins.*
>
> Colossians 1:13–14

Micah wrote, *"You will cast all their sins into the depths of the sea"* (Micah 7:19).

On January 23, 1960, history was made as a two-man crew descended to the deepest known point on the Earth's surface. The Challenger Deep, 35,800 feet below the surface, had been conquered. If the highest mountain on earth was to be dropped into this trench, it would still be covered by over one mile of water.

God dealt with the sin issue so we don't need to. We can't get to forgiveness on our own! It's out of reach, so why go back to the past? Sin is a burden we can't possibly deal with, but when we confess our sin *"He is faithful and righteous to forgive us our sins and to cleanse us from all unrighteousness"* (1 John 1:9).

I've heard some say, "When I get my act together, I'll come to God." Sorry, but you'll never make it. When someone is seriously sick or injured, they don't wait until they recover before going to the hospital. You get to the one who can help you as soon as possible. Jesus Christ came to help a seriously sin-sick world by taking the punishment that was due you and me.

When John the Baptist saw Jesus coming to him, he said, *"Behold, the Lamb of God who takes away the sin of the world!"* (John 1:29)

Remember, in Latin the name Jesus means "God is salvation." What amazing love! God is so willing to pardon that Isaiah 53 tells us it actually pleased him to crush Jesus.

> *But God demonstrates His own love toward us, in that while we were yet sinners, Christ died for us. Much more then, having now been justified by His blood, we shall be saved from the wrath of God through Him.*
>
> Romans 5:8–9

Hallelujah! We worship the creator who pardons.

God Restores

JUST A FEW YEARS AGO, AN ANGRY MAN RAN INTO A MUSEUM IN Amsterdam and headed for Rembrandt's famous painting "Night Watch." He took out a knife and slashed it a number of times before he could be stopped. A short time later, another troubled man slipped into St. Peter's Cathedral in Rome and with a hammer began to smash Michelangelo's sculpture "The Pieta." Two beautiful works of art were severely damaged, but officials didn't throw them out and forget about them. The best experts, working with the utmost care and precision, made every effort to restore the treasures.

Even when damaged, something that is cherished and valuable can be restored and not discarded. That was the message God gave to Israel and to the nations of the world through the prophet Zephaniah. In this short book of three chapters, we read that mankind had effectively damaged the image of God in himself by idolatry and selfishness. God declared that he would judge the wickedness of man, but that's not the end of the story. God also declared that he would restore.

Things were bad. People were sacrificing their children to the Ammonite idol Milcom. The poor were being suppressed by the wealthy. One would be just in destroying such people, but God restores.

Zephaniah 2:3 is God's cry to mankind:

Seek the Lord, all who are humble, and follow his commands. Seek to do what is right and to live humbly. Perhaps even yet the Lord will protect you—protect you from his anger on that day of destruction.

NLT

In Genesis 32, we read that Jacob fought with God. Instead of just destroying this crook, God left him with a limp as a reminder and then changed him into Israel, prince of God.

Yes, we have all sinned and come short of the glory of God, but he doesn't give up on anyone. The last three verses of Zephaniah record God's promise to restore. No matter how we have marred God's image in us by sin, he desires to restore us. Praise God!

Peter said,

Therefore repent and return, so that your sins may be wiped away, in order that times of refreshing may come from the presence of the Lord; and that He may send Jesus, the Christ appointed for you, whom heaven must receive until the period of restoration of all things...

Acts 3:19–21

Peter was speaking to Jews. Even hundreds of years later, God hadn't given up on Israel. His mercy for the rebelliousness is remarkable. God isn't willing that anyone should perish. The apostle Paul wrote that God *"desires all men to be saved and to come to the knowledge of the truth"* (1 Timothy 2:4). We were created for relationship with the creator, so restoration is not just health or wealth; more importantly, it's the kind of relationship God had with mankind in the garden before sin. You and I may be damaged goods, but God considers us his masterpieces. He desires to restore his beauty in us. If we will only humbly bow to him and repent, he will do amazing things. His heart of love calls us to respond to him.

God Sees

NOTHING IS HIDDEN FROM GOD. HIS KNOWLEDGE OF EVERY DETAIL IS complete. The psalmist said, *"Behold, O Lord, You know it all"* (Psalm 139:4). Later in the chapter, David makes an invitation:

> *Search me, O God, and know my heart; try me and know my anxious thoughts; and see if there be any hurtful way in me, and lead me in the everlasting way.*
>
> Psalm 139:23–24

God doesn't need an invitation to look into our lives, but we desperately need him to. He already sees, but we can't always see. His knowledge of every part of our lives is remarkable because he saw it all. He can reveal to us the things he sees so that we can confess, repent, be cleansed, and be healed.

God sees all that happens to us that shapes the way we think, how we act, and how we react. Lest we think that he's just looking through a cloud from a lofty position like a disconnected monarch, we are assured that God sees with an eye to help (Psalm 46:1).

One important thing God is looking for is a willingness to ac-knowledge him and the salvation he freely offers. David also wrote,

"The Lord has looked down from heaven upon the sons of men to see if there are any who understand, who seek after God" (Psalm 14:2).

God isn't ignorant of our troubles. He knows about each one and is patiently waiting to love us through it all. It's up to all mankind to join David in his cry to God in Psalm 139:23–24. If we recognize who Creator God is and his great compassion for us, we won't try to hide and then blame him for our feelings of abandonment. We'll cry out to him, "O God, see what happened to me! Help!"

God's eyes see deep into our lives. Sometimes we can hide sin from others, but we can never hide from him. John the Revelator said, *"His eyes were like a flame of fire"* (Revelation 1:14). He doesn't condone sin in us. His eyes burn with righteous anger. We are wise to not follow the lead of Adam and Eve, but to confess what he has already seen.

The greatness of God to see all, and yet reach out in love, is beyond words.

God Speaks

ONE DAY, GOD WAS WALKING IN THE GARDEN OF EDEN. HE CALLED out to Adam, *"Where are you?"* (Genesis 3:9) Although Adam and Eve had just disobeyed him, he didn't say, "You sinners! I know what you just did. How stupid can you be?" No, instead he called out to reconcile them.

Read again the account of Genesis 3 and see how determined God was to reach them. This is the way God speaks. The voice of God to his creation is unmistakable. Even when there was no matter of any kind, he spoke and a billion times a billion worlds were created (Genesis 1:3–24). His voice spoke through Jesus, and the winds and waves of a storm died down (Luke 8:22–25). He spoke and bodies were healed (Matthew 8:5–13). Creation listens and responds when God speaks.

In Hebrews 12:1, we are reminded that God speaks to us through Jesus. Can you hear what he's saying? "I love you. I forgive you. Come fellowship with me. You are precious to me. Do not be afraid." Instead of words of condemnation, God says through Jesus, *"I do not condemn you"* (John 8:11), just as he did to the woman caught in adultery and to the crook Zaccheus, when Jesus said, *"[T]oday I must stay at your house"* (Luke 19:5).

Even when hanging on the cross, Jesus spoke life to a thief, who responded to him in faith and said, *"Truly I say to you, today you shall be with Me in paradise"* (Luke 23:43). His determination to speak life to the man was greater than his pain. That is the nature of the voice of God.

In a world full of voices, we do well to listen for God's words. His is a giving voice for a desperate people. Daily he calls out, *"Come to Me, all who are heavy-laden, and I will give you rest"* (Matthew 11:28). What is he saying to you today?

God Touches

THE BIBLE TELLS US THAT HE FORMED MAN, WHEREAS OTHER PARTS of his creation came into existence when he spoke (Genesis 2:7). Could that be because he intended a unique and intimate relationship with mankind? Not only did God form man out of the dust, but he has reached out over the centuries. Consider His expressions through the person of Jesus. He touched the leper (Matthew 8:3). He touched someone with a fever (Matthew 8:15). Jesus didn't need to touch them in order to heal them, thus risking transmission of disease to his human body. Jesus also touched the blind eyes (Matthew 9:29) and the deaf ears (Mark 7:33) with those caring hands.

God's hands are strong, but also gentle. They show the unmatched love we all need.

This has always been God's way toward us. He reaches out with love and invites us into relationship. Out of a heart of mercy, Jesus, when confronted by the accusers of the adulterous woman, used his hand to write in the sand (John 8:6). His hands also formed a whip to drive out those who interfered with God's desire to commune with people (John 2:13–17). On the cross, Jesus' hands opened wide in love to the nails that were driven through them.

Another beautiful picture of his hands portrays him washing the feet of his disciples (John 13:5). Imagine. When kings and queens, popes, and other important people are approached, their hands are kissed in honor. Jesus, the King of Kings, chose instead to humble himself and wipe the dusty, dirty feet of his friends. Those hands expressed the love of God.

Is there any doubt about God's loving touch? If so, let's look at what God himself says:

Thus says God the Lord, who created the heavens and stretched them out, who spread out the earth and its offspring, who gives breath to the people on it and spirit to those who walk in it, "I am the Lord, I have called you in righteousness, I will also hold you by the hand and watch over you. . ."

Isaiah 42:6

This message to the stubborn and rebellious Israelites shows that God isn't in the habit of crushing people, but restoring and building.

So much more could be said about how God touches, but we do well to remember the words of Jesus in John 10. He tells us,

My sheep hear My voice, and I know them, and they follow Me; and I give eternal life to them, and they will never perish; and no one will snatch them out of My hand.

John 10:27–28

No matter what comes along, God is reaching out to touch us, to heal us, to save us, and to protect us. Hallelujah!

Part Two:
The Manifestations of God

God Is a Person

TRUE WORSHIP IS DUE A PERSON WHO EXISTS, HAS EXISTED BEFORE TIME began, and will long exist after time waves goodbye. This person alone is to be worshipped. No created things, like idols fashioned out of wood or stone, are worthy to be worshipped. This person who alone is to be worshipped is not an "energy force," as new age thinkers have declared. He created human beings in his own image. A force doesn't feel the pain of others, but this person we are speaking of most certainly does. The creator, who transcends anything imaginable, is known as God (from the Anglo-Saxon word "the good").

He has revealed himself to his creation in the most intimate ways. He interacts with his creation. He speaks to his creation (Exodus 3:4, Acts 13:2, Hebrews 1:1, 12:25, among many other references). He has shown his feelings to his creation (Ephesians 4:30, Hebrews 3:17, and once again many more). He has declared his anger to a rebellious creation (Hebrews 3:17, 12:25–28). He has had determined plans that transcend time periods (Isaiah 53, Jeremiah 29:11). He expresses his desires (Hebrews 6:17, John 3:16, 2 Peter 3:9).

God is kind. He hears, he forgives, he guides, he teaches, he encourages, he judges, and he rewards. Only a person can do all this and more.

Though some deny the existence of God and others distort who God is, the fact of who God is can be seen in the undeniable coming of the long-prophesied Messiah (Christ). Jesus gave a face to God. No one can hide behind any excuse.

Minutes before his betrayal and crucifixion, Jesus Christ said to God the Father, *"This is eternal life, that they [all who will have relationship with him] may know You, the only true God, and Jesus Christ whom You have sent"* (John 17:3).

Excusing one's lifestyle because of a belief that God is only a thought or force and not a person isn't only sad but dangerous. Following this life leads to certain judgment before an actual person. Revelation 20 prophetically describes the scene. A person is seen sitting on a throne. This is the same person we read of in the prophesy of Isaiah 6. The one who is worshipped by all created beings is a person.

Contrasting the idolatry that man has committed, Ezra wrote,

Sing to the Lord, all the earth; proclaim good tidings of His salvation from day to day. Tell of His glory among the nations, His wonderful deeds among all the peoples. For great is the Lord, and greatly to be praised; He also is to be feared above all gods. For all the gods of the peoples are idols, but the Lord made the heavens.

I Chronicles 16:23–26

One might also make excuse for why they don't worship God right now. Accepting the lie that God isn't a person without equal is the norm, but someday, *"at the name of Jesus EVERY KNEE WILL BOW, of those who are in heaven and on earth and under the earth"* (Philippians 2:10).

Boldly we proclaim that God is a person who can be known. He has physically healed and changed the lives of countless people, including me!

God Is Able

THE GREEK WORD FOR GOD'S ABILITY IS *DYNAMAI*. WE GET OUR English word dynamite from this root word. God's ability is dynamite! It's powerful in any situation you or I face.

The two verses that precede the book of Revelation are commonly known as a doxology:

> *Now to Him who is able to keep you from stumbling, and to make you stand in the presence of His glory blameless with great joy, to the only God our Savior, through Jesus Christ our Lord, be glory, majesty, dominion and authority, before all time and now and forever. Amen*
>
> Jude 24–25

These verses reveal that God is dynamically able in three specific ways that concern us all.

1. God is able to keep us from stumbling. In mountain climbing, the beginner hiker attaches himself to the expert so that if he loses his footing, he won't stumble and fall to his death. In the same manner, if we keep connected with God, we cannot fall. He keeps us safe.

Notice that God is able to keep us from stumbling, but we can, by our choices, loosen our grip on him. There is a continual negative potential to our wills. We all have the choice to keep our grip on God or simply let go in every situation. The good news is that we are secure in God if we choose to be.

Nothing can separate us from the love of God unless we choose to walk away from God. The word "stumble" here refers to losing one's footing, stumbling, or falling figuratively. Jude was warning his readers about false teachers who were promoting both false doctrine and practicing a sinful lifestyle. The context makes it clear that Jude was encouraging believers to look to the One who could keep them from being duped by false teachers.

If we keep our eyes on the good shepherd, he will lead us in paths of righteousness. Jesus leads his sheep to avoid dangerous routes. (Psalm 23:3)

2. God is able to make us stand. The posture of standing is significant to every human being. In every court room, the accused is instructed to stand and proclaim innocence or guilt, and later the same will stand to receive the judgment of the court. The apostle Paul reminds us that all of us will be in God's court room. We will all stand before the judgment seat of God.

> *For it is written,* "AS I LIVE, SAYS THE LORD, EVERY KNEE SHALL BOW TO ME, AND EVERY TONGUE SHALL GIVE PRAISE TO GOD."
>
> Romans 14:11

Before the one who knows all, we will stand waiting for the righteous judge to speak. Praise God, for he is able to make us stand in that day!

> *. . .for all have sinned and fall short of the glory of God, being justified as a gift by His grace through the redemption which is in Christ Jesus; whom God displayed publicly as a propitiation in His blood through faith. This was to demonstrate His righteousness, because in the forbearance of God He passed over the sins previously committed; for the demonstration, I say, of His righteousness at the present time, so that He would be just and the justifier of the one who has faith in Jesus.*
>
> Romans 3:23–26

3. God is able to make us blameless with great joy. God doesn't make us blameless with any level of frustration. He makes us blameless with great joy! He never says, "This better be the last time." He loves us so much that he makes us blameless with great joy. One of the most popular verses in scripture is found in Nehemiah 8:10. When the people understood how sinful they had been and how far they were from God, they wept. They felt true remorse and they repented. Nehemiah and Ezra told them to stop weeping and to understand that the *"joy of the Lord is [their] strength"* (Nehemiah 8:10).

God joyfully forgives and makes blameless those who believe who he is. In so many wonderful ways, God is dynamically able. No matter how dark our lives have become, simply placing our faith in Jesus Christ ignites the powerful dynamite of God's ability!

God Is Bread

FEEDING THE HUNGRY HAS ALWAYS BEEN A PRIORITY. WITHOUT sustenance, man perishes. All seek food. The thief, the righteous, the infant, the politician, every man and every woman, need and look for food. In the book on belief, the Gospel of John, Jesus fed five thousand (John 6). He did it miraculously. He had no barns or teams of workers to distribute napkins, drinks, and lunches. In his power to do what man cannot do, he made five loaves and two fishes satisfy the crowd.

Later in the same chapter, Jesus contrasted the bread that only lasts for a little while with the bread that lasts forever. Jesus said that the bread that is from heaven gives life to the world. What did Jesus say was this wonderful life-giving food? He said it was none other than himself. *"I am the bread of life; he who comes to Me will not hunger..."* (John 6:35). In case anyone was confused, Jesus made it clear that he was speaking of himself by twice saying that he is the bread of life (John 6:41, 48). It's not just his wonderful words. It's not just his tender actions of love. He made it clear that His very person is what sustains the life of man.

He also said something that caused some of his disciples to turn away from him. In fact, even today his words are a problem for many: *"unless you eat the flesh of the Son of Man and drink His blood, you have no live in yourselves"* (John 6:53). Was he calling for cannibalism? Of course not. We are to take him into our lives, not as a morsel of food, but as the essence of life. This is done by placing faith in God's ability and love as well as turning away from fear and self-protection. Jesus told the crowd in John 6 not to waste time working so hard for that which is only temporary, but rather to pursue food that will settle the famished soul.

Belief that he is God incarnate is our soul's way of eating, and that continues beyond the point of salvation. Man can be easily fooled into believing temporary things will satisfy one's internal hunger.

Only belief in the finished work of Jesus and his constant presence in our lives can give everlasting life. When he gave himself as a sacrifice for all humanity, he became manna from heaven that fed more than five thousand.

God Is Compassionate

ALL CREATION IS CALLED TO WORSHIP THE CREATOR. HE IS SO incredible that it would be difficult to grasp who he is if it weren't for the fact that he has introduced himself to mankind. He introduced himself to Moses, and we can read of the account in Exodus 34.

It is truly amazing that the first thing God reveals about His name (or character) was that He is merciful and compassionate. One might think that God would have revealed his power and strength, but it was his mercy and compassion God wanted Moses to know about.

Israel had sinned against God and broken His covenant with them. They deserved judgment, but God relented. This wasn't just a one-time event. It happened numerous times.

Consider the prayer of Nehemiah.

But they [Israel] became disobedient and rebelled against You, and cast Your law [the Torah] behind their backs [they ignored what God said] and killed Your prophets who had admonished them so that they might return to You, and they committed great blasphemies. Therefore You delivered them into the hand of their oppressors who oppressed them, but when they cried to You in the time of their distress, You heard from heaven, and according to Your great compassion You gave them deliverers who delivered them from the hand of their oppressors. But as soon as they had rest, they did evil again before You; therefore You abandoned them to the hand of their enemies, so that they ruled over them. When they cried again to You, You heard from heaven, and many times You rescued them according to Your compassion, and admonished them in order to turn them back to Your law.

Nehemiah 9:26–29

God's compassion isn't just sympathy. When we see someone in trouble, we can feel bad for them, but God's compassion is so deep that it goes beyond relieving our pain or discomfort. He wanted Moses to know that his compassion was for his people, who rebelled and brought all kinds of trouble on themselves.

Exodus 32 tells us that Moses got so angry at the people that he broke the tablets God made. In contrast, God wanted Moses to know that he was full of compassion and mercy even for people who were setting up and worshipping idols.

There is a place in Australia that has become a favorite spot for those who want to commit suicide. It's a rocky cliff near Sydney Harbor called The Gap. For nearly fifty years, a man named Don Ritchie has lived across the street from The Gap. Don sees it as his responsibility to try to keep people from jumping over. It is estimated that he has saved more than 160 lives by offering conversation, coffee, or tea. In some way, he tries to bring them hope. Don keeps a constant vigil toward the cliff with binoculars. On at least one occasion, a person almost dragged Don over the cliff. He has been described as an angel. Don once said to a reporter, "You can't just sit there and watch them. You gotta try and save them. It's pretty simple."[1]

That's what God does. He watches with compassion and mercy, then does what he can to stop people from destroying themselves.

Aren't you glad that God is compassionate and merciful? He's worthy of all the worship and praise we can offer.

---

1 "Confront suicidal people, local hero says," *Sydney Morning Herald* (Sydney, Australia), January 25, 2011.

God Is Good

A RICH YOUNG RULER ONCE CAME TO JESUS AND ASKED A QUESTION most people might ask if they were in the same position: *"Teacher, what good thing shall I do that I may obtain eternal life?"* (Matthew 19:16) It seems hard for mankind to understand that no amount of rule-keeping will be enough.

Jesus went along with the man and said, *"If you wish to enter into life, keep the commandments."* (Matthew 19:17) The man knew that keeping the commandments wasn't enough, because he said, *"All these I have kept; what am I still lacking?"* (Matthew 19:20) Something told him he was in need.

Jesus went on to tell him what to do, but because of the hold riches had on him, he left Jesus sad. The answer was too difficult for the man. "Give away your riches" wasn't what he expected or wanted to hear. In fact, he didn't really want Jesus to be his Savior. He wanted to be his own Savior.

Jesus said to him, *"There is only One who is good"* (Matthew 19:17), and that's God himself. What an amazing teaching: only God is good! No matter how great our efforts, nothing can compare to the goodness of God. In Mark 10, we are told that Jesus had compassion on this man because he loved him.

The goodness of God doesn't push anyone away. In fact, it's an invitation to closeness. God is good.

Periodically you may hear someone say, "If God is so good, why is there so much trouble in this world?" The simple answer is that trouble doesn't change who God is. God is good. No amount of trouble can change the fact that God is good. *"The Lord is good, a stronghold in the day of trouble..."* (Nahum 1:7).

He would have been just in condemning this world and squashing us like bugs, but no, God is good! In fact, the goodness of God leads us to repentance (Romans 2:4).

God isn't some kind of uncaring meany. He is good. The psalmist wrote, *"The Lord is good to all, and his mercies are over all His works"* (Psalm 145:9).

The goodness of God is wrapped up and packaged in who Jesus Christ is. Though he was sinless, he *"gave Himself for our sins so that He might rescue us from this present evil age, according to the will of our God and Father..."* (Galatians 1:4).

If you're like me, you're thankful that Jesus rescued us from this present evil age! We're also thankful that he rescued us from ourselves. Each and every one of us are so opinionated. The temptation is for us to arrogantly proclaim what is good, but God alone is the arbitrator of what is good.

The goodness of God isn't wrapped up in my convenience or my happiness, otherwise I become the judge of what is good and what is not. God alone is the measure of good. Jesus Christ, the blessed Son of God, made that clear to the rich young ruler.

God is so good. Eternal life is possible.

Satan's deception of Eve distorted the goodness of God by introducing a sinister question to doubt God: *"For God knows that in the day you eat from it [the fruit of the tree] your eyes will be opened, and you will be like God, knowing good and evil"* (Genesis 3:5). If God is good, how can he lie? The deception doesn't change today. If God is so good, how can he let this happen? To entertain these thoughts as truth would be equal to what Eve accepted as truth.

God is good, and no amount of lies can change that. No trouble so great and hideous can change the foundational truth that God is good. One only needs to consider Jesus Christ to know that God is good! We worship God, who alone is good.

God Is Love

THE PROPHET ISAIAH SAID THAT THE MESSIAH WOULD BE A SUFFERING servant (Isaiah 53).

HE WAS DESPISED AND FORSAKEN OF MEN.
HE WAS PIERCED THROUGH FOR OUR TRANSGRESSIONS.
HE WAS CRUSHED FOR OUR INIQUITIES.
HE WAS OPPRESSED.
HE WAS AFFLICTED.

The good news is that Jesus did all this because of God's great plan to redeem us from the mess we made.

By His knowledge the Righteous One, My Servant, will justify the many, as He will bear their iniquities.

Isaiah 53:11

God gave us the amazing gift of choice, but he also had choice! He chose to make a way for us to be restored to relationship with him.

Often when wronged, we will not seek reconciliation, but God did. He made a choice to not only forgive and pay the penalty, but also to search for the lost ones.

God is love. His love extends to all! His love is for the rich, the poor, the blind, the deaf, the happy, the sad, the lonely, the discouraged, and for you and me! God showed his love for us when he sent his only Son into the world to give us life. Real love isn't our love for God, but his love for us. God sent his Son to be the sacrifice by which our sins are forgiven. Dear friends, since God loved us this much, we must love each other (1 John 4:9–11).

When a leper came to him, Jesus reached out His hand to heal him (Mark 1:40). When the thief on the cross cried out, Jesus promised him life (Luke 23:43). When a woman was caught in adultery, Jesus forgave (John 8:11). When faced with great personal suffering, Jesus obeyed the father and prayed, *"Yet not as I will, but as You will"* (Matthew 26:39). God's choices have always been birthed out of his love for each soul that has or will ever live. This is why I worship him and serve him! He has taught us to choose love first! When it's not easy, when people aren't deserving, or when we have to make a tough choice, we only need to look to God as our example.

The cost was never a factor in the decisions God has made. He paid the cost no matter what it was! Imagine the cost of patience that God has for mankind. It's staggering to think that generation after generation has passed with God continuing to reach out to all with loving arms.

Christ arrives right on time to make this happen. He didn't, and doesn't, wait for us to get ready. He presented himself for this sacrificial death when we were far too weak and rebellious to do anything to get ourselves ready. And even if we hadn't been so weak, we wouldn't have known what to do anyway. We can understand someone dying for a person worth dying for, and we can understand how someone good and noble could inspire us to selfless sacrifice. But God put his love on the line for us by offering his Son in sacrificial death while we were of no use whatever to him.

Romans 5:6–8, The Message

I am so grateful for God's loving choice!

God Is Near

ALL WE KNOW ABOUT GOD IS WRAPPED UP IN THE FACT THAT HE IS near. The apostle Paul wrote,

> *Rejoice in the Lord always; again I will say, rejoice! Let your gentle spirit be known to all men. The Lord is near. Be anxious for nothing, but in everything by prayer and supplication with thanksgiving let your requests be made known to God. And the peace of God, which surpasses all comprehension, will guard your hearts and your minds in Christ Jesus.*
> Philippians 4:4–7

The context of this is that God is literally near. This verse is not about the second coming. God does walk through life with you and me.

Imagine that the creator of all that is, the one who knows all things and is all-powerful, is near you and me. That's enough to get the party started! Rejoice in the Lord always! God is close! He's not disconnected from you! All that God is—the guide, the deliverer, the teacher, the shelter, the help, and much more—is within reach.

The writer of Hebrews says, *"[L]et us draw near with a sincere heart in full assurance of faith, having our hearts sprinkled clean from an evil conscience and our bodies washed with pure water"* (Hebrews 11:22).

Scripture has much to say about the nearness of God.

> *The Lord is near to the brokenhearted and saves those who are crushed in spirit. Many are the afflictions of the righteous, but the Lord delivers him out of them all.*
>
> Psalms 34:18–19

> *The Lord is near to all who call upon Him, to all who call upon Him in truth. He will fulfill the desire of those who fear Him; He will also hear their cry and will save them.*
>
> Psalms 145:18–19

> *God is our refuge and strength, a very present help in trouble.*
>
> Psalms 46:1

> *You will make known to me the path of life; in Your presence is fullness of joy; in Your right hand there are pleasures forever.*
>
> Psalm 16:11

Since God is present everywhere, when we talk about the presence of God, we're really talking about the realization of God's presence, the perception of His presence, becoming conscious of His presence.

During the 1930s, 250 men held the ropes to an airship to prevent it from floating away. Suddenly a gust of wind caught one end of the airship high off the ground. Some of the men immediately let go of their ropes and fell safely to the ground. Others panicked, clinging firmly. Several men who couldn't keep holding fell and were seriously injured. One man, however, continued to dangle high in the air for forty-five minutes until he was rescued. Reporters later asked him how he was able to hold on to the rope for so long: "I didn't hold on to the rope," he replied. "I just tied it around my waist, and the rope held on to me."[2]

Instead of trying to hold on to God, let God hold on to you. He can be trusted! He is near and is able to handle all that concerns us.

> *Rejoice in the Lord always; again I will say, rejoice! Let your gentle spirit be known to all men. The Lord is near. Be anxious for nothing. . .*
> Philippians 4:4-6

In the original Greek text, there is no period between "The Lord is near" and "Be anxious for nothing."[3] So the bottom line is: Party! Rejoice! And again I say, party! God is near! The burden-bearer, the bread of life, the storm-chaser, the righteous judge, the thirst quencher, and friend that is closer than a brother!

---

2 Kent Crockett, *I Once Was Blind But Now I Squint* (Chattanooga, TN: AMG Publishers, 2004), 138.

3 Greek New Testaments show punctuation, but original manuscripts do not include any punctuation.

God Is Relational

THERE IS A STRIKING CONTRAST BETWEEN THE CREATOR AND THE created gods of men. The one and only living God is relational. Idols that men set up are not relational.

This is remarkable because people of great power and authority are usually the least approachable, whereas God, who is above everything, longs for us to reach out to him. He wants all of his creation to be in relationship with him. How marvelous is that! Let's take it one step further: if it wasn't for his initiation and pursuit of us, we wouldn't pay any attention to him and could never know him.

God made us not only to want and need relationship with other human beings, but with the capacity to know him. Imagine! God wants relationship with you and me. Amazing! God has no needs. He is self-sustaining and could have anything he wants. Yet, as unfathomable as this is, he wants to know us.

This relationship with God is not a casual one, either. He knows all about us. He knows every cell of our bodies. He knows our thoughts and what we will say before we even say it (Psalm 139:4). By his great and loving power, he holds us together (Colossians 1:17, Hebrews 1:3). He knows us by name! That's right! He knows all who live or who have ever lived by name!

The million dollar question that every human being must be asked is, "Do you know the one and only God of Creation?" Relationship with God is the most important part of life. In fact, it is so important that God became angry with King Solomon because his heart was turned away from the Lord. God had revealed himself twice to Solomon (1 Kings 11:9), but scripture makes it clear that Solomon still went after other gods (1 Kings 11:10).

Even Adam and Eve missed the point. Certainly, they were complete and intact human beings made in their creator's image, but they failed to run to him in the time of their temptation and lost out on relationship. Sadly, all of us have done the same thing (Isaiah 53:5).

There will be a reckoning day for our rejection of him, but in the meantime he reaches out with great love and mind-boggling patience (John 3:16–18). At one time in his life, Solomon wrote,

Blessed be the Lord God, the God of Israel, who alone works wonders. And blessed be His glorious name forever; and may the whole earth be filled with His glory.

Psalm 72:18–19

Solomon knew who God is. He also said, *"He will have compassion on the poor and needy, and the lives of the needy he will save"* (Psalm 72:13). His downfall came when his heart wasn't wholly devoted to the Lord his God (1 Kings 11:4).

Relationship with God isn't casual, but complete devotion— and isn't that just a reflection of his image? He is completely devoted to us, his creation!

Part Three:
Who God is to Me

God Is My Anchor

WE LIVE IN A WORLD OF GREAT SHAKING. LITERALLY AND FIGURATIVELY, things move with great force. Over five hundred thousand earthquakes take place each year, and as terrible as they are, people experience personal shaking that seems much worse. Cancer, AIDS, financial ruin, unimaginable accidents, and the death of loved ones blindside the unsuspecting. Right when the sky is blue and the bank account is full, trouble comes.

At the church I pastor, I often say, "When trouble comes to your door, introduce it to Jesus Christ." No matter what level of seismic activity in our lives, *"we have as an anchor of the soul, a hope both sure and steadfast. . ."* (Hebrews 6:19). Earlier in Hebrews, we read that God spoke to humanity in His Son: *"And He is the radiance of His glory and the exact representation of His nature, and upholds all things by the word of His power"* (Hebrews 1:3). The analogy of an anchor is apt when storms surround, but our anchor isn't to the ground but heavenward. He, Jesus, *"upholds all things by the word of His power."*

In Jesus Christ, we are receiving *"a kingdom which cannot be shaken"* (Hebrews 12:28). Yes, the world around us can be shaking, but because our anchor is the Son of God we have assurance that we are safe.

The writer of Hebrews gives us a caution to *"not refuse Him who is speaking"* (Hebrews 12:25). We only hurt ourselves by figuratively putting our fingers in our ears. Jesus is our high priest (Hebrews 3:1–6), the only mediator between God and man (Hebrews 9:15), our example (Hebrews 12:1–3), our great shepherd (Hebrews 13:20), and he doesn't change (Hebrews 13:8).

No matter the problem, sin, or pain, we are wise to fix *"our eyes on Jesus, the author and perfecter of faith, who for the joy set before Him endured the cross, despising the shame, and has sat down at the right hand of the throne of God"* (Hebrews 12:2). So, *"let us continually offer up a sacrifice of praise to God, that is, the fruit of lips that give thanks to His name"* (Hebrews 13:15).

The flesh may say, "I can't praise God right now. It's too hard." He understands and loves us even when those thoughts come, but doubts disappear in the midst of our praise! Paul the apostle knew a little about this.

> *Five times I received from the Jews thirty-nine lashes. Three times I was beaten with rods, once I was stoned, three times I was shipwrecked, a night and a day I have spent in the deep.*
> 2 Corinthians 11:24–25

He goes on to tell us about more shaking that he endured. He also said,

> *Therefore we do not lose heart, but though our outer man is decaying, yet our inner man is being renewed day by day. For momentary, light affliction is producing for us an eternal weight of glory far beyond all*

comparison, while we look not at the things which are seen, but at the things which are not seen.

2 Corinthians 4:16–18

The truth is that we live in a fallen world where trouble rains down on all. The difference is that those who anchor their lives to Jesus Christ make it through the temporary struggles in the safety of his care.

Shaking may happen at any moment, but that doesn't intimidate those who place their trust in God. No one knows better than God how we feel, and that's precisely why we worship him while storms batter against us.

As the old hymn says,

We have an anchor that keeps the soul
Steadfast and sure while the billows roll,
Fastened to the Rock which cannot move,
Grounded firm and deep in the Savior's love.[4]

---

4 "Will Your Anchor Hold," Priscilla Jane Owens, 1882.

God Is My Burden-Bearer

PEOPLE KNOW US FOR MORE THAN OUR PHYSICAL APPEARANCE. THEY know us by things that cannot be seen. Often it's our response to a situation in life. When problems take place, we may lose control or become impatient! As we grow in relationship to God, we become less reactive. We learn that God is in control, that he is with us and knows what to do. This calms us and reassures us. Our character then becomes softer. As Christians, we learn that the tests, trials, and problems we face are only temporary. We also learn that God has made very special promises. Jesus told us that he would bear the burdens of those who come to him (Matthew 11:28–29). What a wonderful thing!

If you're like me, your first response to a challenge is to try and think of a way to get out of it, but Jesus said, "Come to me." The reason we are to go to Jesus is that he is all-powerful and has all the information. We are limited in what we can do, but he is not! Added to that is the truth that God is the one who frees us from the weight of sin. Why carry a heavy burden of sin? What will it do but eventually destroy us?

David wrote a psalm of praise that we can meditate on: *"Blessed be the Lord, who daily bears our burden, the God who is our salvation"* (Psalm 68:19).

David was a sinner. Most of us will never commit such grievous sins as David did. He had a man murdered so that he could take the man's wife. David had to live with the effects of this terrible sin, but he saw that God could, would, and did forgive and free him from the burden of sin.

If you struggle with pet sins or tend to carry the problems of life, I have good news for you. Jesus said, *"Come to me, all who are weary and heavy-laden, and I will give you rest"* (Matthew 11:28).

God is your burden-bearer. He has very wide and strong shoulders to carry whatever you are facing and whatever you will face! So give to Jesus what concerns you. Meditate on the truth of who God is and worship him. He is your burden-bearer!

God Is My Comfort

IF YOU HAVEN'T SAID IT, YOU MAY HAVE HEARD SOMEONE ELSE ASK, "Why did God let this happen?" An aching heart might cry out, "Why didn't God do something about this?" Both questions are legitimate. After all, if God did something, then he wouldn't need to comfort us. Practically, God could make a perfect world and there would be no necessity for him to be my comfort.

The sad fact is that God did make a perfect world, and by man's choice, sin entered into every part of life.

Therefore, just as through one man sin entered into the world, and death through sin, and so death spread to all men, because all sinned.

Romans 5:12

Before we lay all the responsibility on Adam and Eve, let's remind ourselves that scripture tells us that all of us hold personal responsibility. (Romans 3:23)

The creator made the perfect situation for humanity to enjoy life, but even before sin entered into the world, God was the comforter. Problems don't need to be present for God to be our comfort. *"Jesus Christ is the same yesterday and today and forever."* (Hebrew 13:8)

God does much more than sooth us when things go wrong. He strengthens us in and through the challenges of life. The Greek word used in 2 Corinthians 1:3 is *paraklesis*. As it is used in reference to God, it means that God strengthens and helps us to be brave.

God wipes away our tears out of his bountiful love, but he also goes further. He does so by helping us face the problems in his strength. Picture God as the one who sympathizes with how we feel but also cares enough not to leave us in pain.

David knew much about the comfort of God. He wrote,

> *Even though I walk through the valley of the shadow of death, I fear no evil, for You [God the Good Shepherd] are with me; Your rod and Your staff, they comfort me.*
>
> Psalm 23:4

Up until this verse, Psalm 23 looks pretty good for sheep under the care of the Good Shepherd. Now life sets in with dark and foreboding problems. The first three verses focus on the shepherd, but now the personal pronoun "I" shows up.

Isn't that like life for you and me? We can worship God because of his loving care and for who he is, but when troubles come we're tempted to look away from him and more at ourselves. The fact is that God didn't suddenly run away or hide. He's there even in the dangers and heartaches, and he comforts us so we can keep walking through life with him.

The rod and staff used by the Good Shepherd are more than weapons against our enemies. They are also tools to guide us when we get off-track. This can happen quickly when our focus becomes wrapped around our circumstances. Sometimes God has to comfort us by getting our attention. He wants to comfort us with the reality of who he is.

Problems cannot solve themselves, but God, my encouragement, my burden-bearer, my hope, my help, and my guide is the one who comforts me.

On a cold winter night, it's always great to snuggle up with a nice blanket. God is more than just a blanket. He's the one who gives us courage as we focus on him. He is my comforter.

God Is My Confidence

I ALWAYS LIKE TO PROJECT MY THOUGHTS INTO THE FUTURE. FOR instance, I like to guess at what I'll be doing and where I'll be in years to come. Two years ago, I wouldn't have guessed I would be living in Singapore. Wow! We certainly don't know our days, but God does.

Psalm 37:18 says, *"The Lord knows the days of the blameless, and their inheritance will be forever."* The verse before it says that *"the Lord sustains the righteous"* (Psalm 37:17). Awesome! In a world where anything can happen, it sure is good to know that God has our backs! He's the one we can keep our confidence in. Meditate on the fact that God is your confidence. In fact, be very suspicious of anything that contradicts what God says in his Word.

The apostle Paul said that *"we are the true circumcision, who worship in the Spirit of God and glory in Christ Jesus and put no confidence in the flesh. . ."* (Philippians 3:3). Paul was one who could boast! He had many things going for him, but he gave it all up. He said, *"But whatever things were gain to me, those things I have counted as loss for the sake of Christ"* (Philippians 3:7). Paul could see that trusting God is a sure thing!

Many things will take place in your life this coming year. Instead of falling back on what you know, what you have, or what you can do, choose to focus on Jesus and place your confidence in him who will never disappoint!

God Is My Defender

WE WORSHIP A GOD WHO DEFENDS. ONE OF THE BEAUTIFUL THINGS about God is that wrapped up in his defense of man is his power, his grace, his love, and his mercy. God defends out of strength and character. He defends not because of our worth, but because of who he is.

Conversely, Satan is the accuser (Revelation 12:10). Scripture tells us that he does this day and night. In other words, he doesn't stop. The good news is that we have a defender who treats us with great love.

Movies and television series often depict defense lawyers of criminals. Their duty is to squash the charges brought against their clients. Theirs is a difficult job. They must often answer condemning evidence. When the guilty verdict is pronounced, the defense loses.

Almighty God is holy and just in all his ways, yet never loses a case as a defender, even though the evidence against all humanity seems insurmountable.

All of us like sheep have gone astray. . .

Isaiah 53:6

. . .for all have sinned and fall short of the glory of God. . .

Romans 3:23

Everyone has chosen to sin and are guilty, but God will gladly defend anyone who places themselves in his hands. How does he do this? Not by winking at sin, but by doing something about it! Hallelujah! Before we come to God, we have no hope. There is no way out. Judgment is our only future, but God came to our defense and was punished on our behalf.

In John 8, we read a wonderful story of when Jesus came to the defense of a guilty woman. The crowd was ready to bring the death sentence down upon her. There was no hope because she had been caught in the very act.

Incidentally, all of us are in a similar position. We are caught because a holy God has been present when we willingly sinned. One of the most well-known scriptures is taken from this story: *"He who is without sin among you, let him be the first to throw a stone at her"* (John 8:7). The scribes and Pharisees were testing Jesus. They wanted to catch him. In order to be just, he had to agree with the law, but what of his love for sinners? They were saying this, testing him, so that they might have grounds for accusing Him (John 8:6). They put Jesus in the place of a judge when Jesus Christ came to earth to be the defender. Oh yes, he is the righteous judge, but praise God, he is also the defender of mankind.

In the case of the woman caught in adultery, Jesus made a glorious statement: *"I do not condemn you, either. Go. From now on sin no more"* (John 8:11). God defends not because we are sinless, but because he already paid the penalty.

68

Some have wondered what Jesus wrote in the sand as the accusers stood over him. Some think he listed the sins of the accusers who were looking on. We don't know, but I wonder if he simply drew a cross.

God Is My Encouragement

WHEN YOU THINK OF SOMEONE WHO'S AN ENCOURAGER, WHO IS BETTER than God? To sinners, to his disciples, or to anyone, Jesus gave hope! The root word for encourage is "courage." To encourage someone is to give that person a level of hope that will give them the courage to face whatever is before them. Jesus gives us hope like no else can. The reason is that he knows our days. He wants us to know that we can! The enemy, the flesh, and this world would tell you that you can't make it. It's too tough.

Let me ask you a question: what is too tough for God? If you and I are hidden in Jesus, there's nothing you cannot do! He gives you the *dunamis*—the power—to face anything. The Lord said to his disciples, *"Do not let your heart be troubled"* (John 14:1). Jesus said this right after telling Peter that he would deny him. Wow! Doesn't that encourage you? Jesus wanted his disciples to know that even though there would be difficulties, they were to choose to be hopeful. Why? The same verse goes on to say, "Believe in God, believe also in Me."

Celebrate the God who is with you! Keep your eyes on the one who will encourage you in all that happens. You can make it with Jesus, the great encourager of your soul!

God Is My Father

JESUS TAUGHT HIS DISCIPLES TO PRAY AND SAID, *"OUR FATHER..."* (Matthew 6:9). He spoke so affectionately of God the Father as he told people that Father God hears, sees, forgives, and provides for the needs of his children. It is truly wonderful to know God as Father.

Conveniently, people will say, "We are all gods." This is plainly false. God is the maker of all. He created, but there's a difference between "maker" and "Father." Jesus made this plain when he answered Jews who argued with him. They spoke of their lineage but didn't recognize that a father is more than just a maker.

"Abraham is our father," said the Jews (John 8:39). Jesus told them that if they were really children of Abraham, they would *do the deeds of Abraham* (John 8:39). The "deeds of Abraham" were no more and no less than simple faith in God. It was Abraham who believed *"God is able"* (Hebrews 11:19), and he passed the test of faith.

Jesus went on to say,

> *But as it is you are seeking to kill Me, a man who has told you the truth, which I heard from God; this Abraham did not do. You are doing the deeds of your father.*

John 8:40–41

The Jews didn't like this, because they knew what he was saying. We aren't all of the same father. The Jews said to Jesus, *"We were not born of fornication; we have one Father; God"* (John 8:41).

What a scene! It was getting pretty hot, but Jesus didn't let it go.

> *If God were your Father, you would love Me, for I proceeded forth and have come from God, for I proceeded forth and have come from God, for I have not even come on My own initiative, but he sent Me. Why do you not understand what I am saying? It is because you cannot hear My word. You are of your father the devil and you want to do the desires of your father.*
>
> John 8:42–44

Jesus taught us about Fatherhood. He told Nicodemus,

> *God so loved the world that he gave his only begotten Son, that whoever believes in Him shall not perish but will have everlasting life.*
>
> John 3:16

Before speaking this well-known statement, Jesus said to Nicodemus, *"That which is born of the flesh is flesh and that which is born of the Spirit is spirit"* (John 3:6).

Being a child of God means that we will be like our Father.

God the Father is not like earthly father who procreates. John wrote,

Now little children, abide in Him, so that when He appears, we may have confidence and not shrink away from Him in shame at His coming. If you know that He is righteous, you know that everyone also who practices righteousness is born of Him. See how great a love the Father has bestowed on us, that we would be called children of God; and such we are.

I John 2:28–3:1

Jesus knew about God the Father. He spoke of him as "My Father" (such as in John 15). God is the Father of those who are born of the spirit, so that they also can say "My Father." Everyone can be children of Father God, but the key is listen to the words of Jesus when he said, *"I am the way, the truth, and the life; no one comes to the Father but through Me"* (John 14:6).

Paul told the Romans that as children of God, we can cry out to God as our Papa, Daddy, or Father (Romans 8:15) who frees his kids from fear. No one is like God my Father!

God Is My Friend

I'M SURE YOU KNOW THE VERSE THAT SAYS, *"YOU ARE MY FRIENDS IF YOU do whatever I command you"* (John 15:14). In this passage, there is certainly a condition to Jesus calling us friends, but we're short-sighted if we focus on our side of the agreement and not revel in the ways in which Jesus expresses His friendship to us.

Let's look at how Jesus is our friend as we partner with him! In Luke 7:34, Jesus quoted the Pharisees. They said that Jesus was a friend of sinners. Wow! Isn't that great? I can tell you that I'm glad Jesus saw me, loved me, and wanted to be my friend. When you look for a friend, you usually look for the best in someone, but Jesus loved us in spite of what and who we were.

I have many friends around the world. I treasure them all. Jesus treasures us as his friends. The Bible tells us that he prays for us, that he's preparing a place for us, and not only that but that he walks with us. I miss my friends, but my greatest friend is with me always!

We guard friendship because it means someone really does care about us. Jesus guards our friendship, and so should we. Keep your eyes on your friend, Jesus Christ! Meditate on him and talk to him as you would any other friend. Remember, he is your best friend! No one can compare to him.

God Is My Guide

THE WORSHIP OF GOD IS MORE THAN A MOMENTARY EVENT. WE GO through life with our Savior. He doesn't just point out the way home; he goes with us. He is our guide.

Have you ever felt lost? Has life been confusing? That's why we do well to daily keep our eyes on the Great Guide. His knowledge of all things, especially of us, is complete. Nothing is hidden from his eye, and his wisdom is unfathomable.

In Psalm 32, David writes from man's perspective for the first seven verses. He rejoices in the salvation God gives us. He also declares that God is a hiding place and that he preserves and delivers us in troubled times. David then writes from God's perspective. He writes, *"I will instruct you and teach you in the way which you should go; I will counsel you with My eye upon you"* (Psalm 32:8). He doesn't look to a map for directions. His perfect understanding gives us the advice we need.

Amazingly, God sees each person individually and is more than capable of guiding us all at the same time. God treats us with tender loving care. He satisfies completely so that as sheep we lie down in green pastures. He calms us by leading us beside quiet water (Psalm 23:2). He takes us down the right paths (Psalm 23:3), even as our companion through the dark times (Psalm 23:4), in the very sight of our enemies (Psalm 23:5). God guides us into rest, peace, comfort, life, and most of all into his presence. He gives us freedom from fear, tension, and irritation.

Forging ahead through this life is foolishness and only slows our progress toward our ultimate destination. Isaiah prophesied about Jesus, saying,

> *Who has directed the Spirit of the Lord, or as His counselor has informed Him? With whom did He consult and who gave Him understanding? And who taught Him in the path of justice and taught Him knowledge and informed Him of the way of understanding?*
>
> Isaiah 40:13–14

God is the best, and really the only one qualified to guide us.

Thomas, one of Jesus's disciples, asked, *"[H]ow do we know the way?"* (John 14:5) Jesus explained that getting there is accomplished only by following him: *"I am the way, and the truth, and the life; no one comes to the Father but through Me"* (John 14:6). This is such a comfort, since he is the Great Guide.

So, the next time we feel confused and lost, let's worship God, keep our eyes on Jesus, and follow the Great Guide.

God Is My Help

EACH ONE OF US HAS CRIED OUT FOR HELP AT ONE TIME OR ANOTHER. Sometimes we just need someone to help us with minor assistance. Other times, we're in great need. Circumstances can hit us with a ferocity that seems insurmountable. How can I make it through this? Somebody, help!

The psalmist wrote a song that describes the nature of God to help:

> *I look up to the mountains—does my help come from there? My help comes from the Lord, who made the heavens and the earth! He will not let you stumble and fall; the one who watches over you will not sleep. Indeed, he who watches over Israel never tires and never sleeps. The Lord himself watches over you! The Lord stands beside you as your protective shade. The sun will not hurt you by day, nor the moon at night. The Lord keeps you from all evil and preserves your life. The Lord keeps watch over you as you come and go, both now and forever.*
>
> Psalm 121, NLT

Let's focus on the following three truths about God.

My help comes from the Lord, who made heaven
and earth.
He will not allow your foot to slip.
He who keeps you will not slumber.

Notice that the one who can help is the one who made heaven and earth! I don't know about you, but I'm truly excited by this thought. The one who created all that exists is more than able to handle the problem I'm facing. There's no need to fear tests and trials that can overtake us when we settle on the fact that God, the Maker, can fix it all. Nothing is impossible with God, the Maker of heaven and earth. Just when it seems like the end has come, we can be encouraged to trust that God is able!

Secondly, we can remember that God won't allow our foot to slip. I grew up battling icy sidewalks. Sometimes it was so dangerous that I would walk slowly and deliberately. In a life with many pitfalls and dangers, we are wise to walk slowly and deliberately. God will keep us from falling if we are careful to listen to his cautions.

Finally, God will keep us faithfully and completely. While all of us must sleep, God isn't in need of sleep. He is always and forever aware of my needs and yours.

I Peter 1:5 reminds us that we *are protected by the power of God through faith for a salvation ready to be revealed in the last time."*

Are God's people entitled to trial-free lives? Of course not! We all know there will be times that we need help. Isn't it good to know that we know the one who created all things, will keep us from falling, and is always and forever watching over us? The key is for us to keep our eyes on our Help!

God Is My Hope

IMAGINE: GOD IS MY HOPE! SOME SAY THAT GETTING MARRIED, learning a degree, or making a good living is our hope. One of my favorite songs is "Jesus, Hope of the Nations." Yes, the music is good, but the words are so positive. That's the thing about hope: it's positive. That which we hope for apart from God can be good and positive, but what if it doesn't happen? Does our world come crashing down? You see, hope in God will not disappoint.

The psalmist said, *"No one whose hope is in you will ever be put to shame..."* (Psalm 25:3, NIV). Just look at why it's logical to hope in God and not things:

> *But the eyes of the Lord are on those who fear him, on those whose hope is in his unfailing love... We wait in hope for the Lord; he is our help and our shield.*
>
> Psalm 33:18, 20, NIV

> *...those who hope in the Lord will inherit the land.*
>
> Psalm 37:9, NIV

You are my refuge and my shield; I have put my hope in your word.
Psalm 119:114, NIV

We can be people of hope because God sees us, because he is our help and shield, because we will receive from him as a child from a parent, and because he protects us from everything. The hope we have in a loving, caring, and all-powerful God is the kind of hope that will not fade over time.

If you're like me, you know that things come and go. They are unpredictable. God is not only predictable, he is dependable. He doesn't change like things do. He is good today and he will be good tomorrow.

God Is My Joy

THE MIDDLE CHAPTER OF THE BIBLE, PSALM 118, IS A GREAT EXPRESSION of joy. As you read it, can't you just sense the psalmist bubbling and gushing? *"Give thanks to the Lord, for He is good... Oh let Israel say, 'His lovingkindness is everlasting'"* (Psalm 118:1–2). He couldn't help but say something equal to our expression of "Whoa!" or "Wow!" Joy will do that to you.

The psalmist goes on to say, *"The Lord is for me; I will not fear"* (Psalm 118:6). You and I can say the same. God's lovingkindness is everlasting, and he is for us! In light of who God is, fear need not be a part of our thinking. The thing we must see in scripture is the character of God. God isn't selective in love and kindness. Because he is love, he is kindness.

We cannot comprehend the greatness of God. But we *can* know that he is so wonderful that it brings joy. The reason the psalmist could say, *"In Your presence is fullness of joy"* (Psalm 16:11), is that the magnificence of who God is creates real joy. The good news is that everyone can know this joy, not because of what we do but because of who God is.

Want joy? Live your life in the presence of God, because God is so wonderful. It would be silly to command someone to be joyful.

Instead, I want to invite you to a place where you will experience great joy, walking with the creator of all that is.

Better than looking for the next thing that can give temporary stimulation, let's pursue Almighty God with passion. He is forever the same. He has always been and forever will be good. He even calls us to have a deep meaningful relationship with himself. There is fleeting pleasure in things, but they are only temporary and cannot compare to the magnitude of joy when the creature is friends with its creator.

Imagine the incredible joy you and I will have in experiencing friendship with God, who created a billion times a billion worlds. Who know what he is up to even now? Jesus said, *"I go to prepare a place for you"* (John 14:2). Can you imagine that the creator still continues to create, just for you and me, His children? He is truly beyond all words. He is truly the God who is our joy.

God Is My Master

WHEN YOU THINK OF A MASTER, WHAT'S THE FIRST THING THAT ENTERS your mind? Could it be visions of slave traders beating defenseless servants? Is your perception based on the actions of men toward other men? Unfortunately, if that's the case, you might have a misconception of God as a master.

Remember, God is not an abuser of man but the lover of all who have lived or ever will live. The Bible tells us that sin and death are masters of huge proportion, but Jesus has redeemed us. Imagine! People serve the masters of sin and death. It's not exactly a promising thing to serve destruction! Thankfully, we have made the choice to change ownership. Think about the master we now serve. He is the one who washes feet! He is the one who touches and heals the leper! He is the one who has made many promises that he will keep! Romans 6:22 says, *"But now having been freed from sin and enslaved to God, you derive your benefit, resulting in sanctification, and the outcome, eternal life."* Let's see: on one hand is death, and on the other hand is eternal life.

Remember that He is master over all creation, with one exception: the heart of man.

His authority and power is offered to all, not with a whip but with love. I don't know about you, but I choose to make Jesus Christ my master!

God Is My Peace

THE WRITER OF HEBREWS CONCLUDED HIS LETTER WITH A PRAYER which beginning with, "Now the God of peace, who brought up from the dead the great Shepherd of the sheep through the blood of the eternal covenant, even Jesus our Lord..." (Hebrews 13:20). We know, therefore, who this God of peace is: our eternal heavenly Father. His power is greater than death itself! This God is able to bring peace to any situation we face. In fact, more often than not, he has given us peace without our awareness or knowledge.

Through the Great Shepherd of the sheep, our God has promised to keep us in perfect peace. There is only one condition to this promise. God's people must keep their minds focused on him. The absence of problems does not equal peace. Many struggle with inner turmoil. You may have often heard that the battleground is in the mind. Temptation and trials are fought with the mind. Believers have peace when their minds are kept on the Lord minute by minute and day by day. It is then that God, who is our peace, fills our lives rather than the circumstances around us.

Someone wisely said, "You are the architect of your day. So, have a good day, unless you have other plans." The formula is simple.

We must keep our minds on God. The choice is ours: will you have a life of turmoil or a life of peace?

God Is My Protector

PRAISE GOD! THE APOSTLE PETER OPENS HIS FIRST LETTER WITH PRAISE and worship as he outlines who God is. He says in 1 Peter 1:3–5 that God has great mercy, that God causes us to be born again to a living hope, and that God protects his people through his power.

These three facts about God are enough to talk about for a long, long time. Wow! This sounds like a great deal! God the Holy Spirit inspired Peter to tell us very good news. We can all use good news. In a world that seems on the brink of disaster and when dangers seem to surround us, it is good news to know that God has great mercy, that he causes us to be born again to a living hope, and that he protects us.

Jesus told throngs of people who were under the oppression of Rome that the fears of this life have only limited powers. Yes, there are great concerns for the body. Pollution, the threat of nuclear war, disease, and economic crisis can bring temporary difficulties, but Jesus encourages us with his words of love.

> Are not five sparrows sold for two cents? Yet not one of them is forgotten before God. Indeed , the very hairs of your head are all numbered. Do not fear; you are more valuable than many sparrows.

> Luke 12:6–7

God is our protector. He knows and cares for us. The great message that we would be wise to hear is that some things are temporary and other things are eternal. God's love and protection for us are eternal. We are kept by the power of God.

Job said,

> As for me, I know that my Redeemer lives, and at the last He will take His stand on the earth. Even after my skin is destroyed, yet from my flesh I shall see God.
>
> Job 19:25–26

Job experienced the truth that although troubles come, in the end God loves and cares.

The question of protection is more than the avoidance of pain and difficulty in this temporal life. The protection God gives his children is beyond the temporary. As his people, we are hidden in Christ. We are protected by his great power.

It warrants repeating that God provides mercy, hope, and protection. He is the Good Shepherd. This is the God we worship. Instead of cursing the darkness, let's worship him.

God Is My Rewarder

RECEIVING A REWARD IS WONDERFUL, A RECOGNITION OF SOMETHING attained or accomplished. Even more significant is the source of the reward. Receiving a reward from the Queen of England is greater than winning a carnival game. It is an honor to be invited to receive from someone of great stature.

Can you imagine what it's like to receive a reward from the creator of all things? That is precisely what happens for those who seek him. Hebrews 11:6 tells us that just seeking God results in a reward from God himself. Seeking God must be a very special task for God to present a reward.

In Hebrews 11, we read about the heroes of faith. These spiritual giants placed their faith in the One who transcends every situation. No matter what happened, they looked for the One who is above all. Some may be tempted to seek God because of some trophy. In doing so, they would be shortsighted. No matter how great the reward given, nothing can compare to God himself. He is the One who spoke a billion times a billion worlds into existence, knows the thoughts of all seven billion inhabitants of the earth, and isn't subject to time or space. Seek God? We would be foolish not to seek him.

God said to Abraham that he (God) was his (Abraham's) reward (Genesis 15:1). Surely Abraham could have considered becoming the father of many nations a prize, but God said otherwise.

Who needs rewards when you have God? A trophy vaporizes like steam when compared to God himself. God is the rewarder, but he is also the reward for those who seek him. The way we seek him is through faith and belief that he *is*, in all areas of life. We ask, "Where is God?" Hebrews 11 says that Abraham looked for God when asked to sacrifice Isaac and found a God who was able *"to raise people even from the dead"* (Hebrews 11:19). When reading and studying scripture, we also seek God by looking for him on every page. Every time we pick up the Bible, our most valuable question is, "What does scripture say about God?"

Have you looked at the vastness of the sky? Worship pours out from God's creation. Sometimes I notice brilliant colors and begin to worship God for what he created. When blessings surprise us, we worship the God of all love. And in difficult times, just like those in Hebrews 11, we worship God in faith. In these ways, we recognize God. This is seeking him in all areas of life. I don't know about you, but my joy is seeking God, both my rewarder and my reward. Any other prize is bonus.

God Is My Shelter

MY MENTOR, DR. GEORGE WESTLAKE, HAS OFTEN PREACHED FROM Psalm 91. It was and continues to be one of my favorite passages of scripture. It was moving to hear him quote this beautiful passage while choking back tears. Tears? Yes, tears! He saw the wonder of God's love in this chapter: *"He who dwells in the shelter of the Most High. . ."* (Psalm 91:1). If one could feast on the word of God, these ten words could feed us for a long, long time.

He (God). We aren't talking about a man or woman who can fail. God is the one whom we adore and magnify, because he is! God said to Moses, *"I AM"* (Exodus 3:14). Our first thought should always and forever be God! There is no other. Perfect in love, perfect in grace, perfect in mercy.

Who dwells. Living in a home is only part of the story. Only a portion of my life is spent there. A dwelling is more than four walls. I have known some who dwell in bitterness and fear. I have also known people who live in the freedom of joy and peace that springs from a sweet relationship with God. Home is where your heart is—that's a true statement. The troubling thing is that some may choose to let their hearts dwell in places God never intended for them.

In the shelter. Have you ever wondered what the shelter of God is? Isn't it great to be in a shelter when the rains come or when winds kick up? Not only do we need shelter for our bodies, we also need shelter for our inner man. This world of hatred and disconnection swirls indiscriminately. The soul of man needs a shelter from what can wound and ultimately destroy.

Of the Most High. The good news is that God is above all. By saying this, it is not inferred that God is afar off. He is the Most High, meaning nothing supersedes his authority and power. He is supremely the great and mighty ruler over all things. Read the book of Job, look at the blue sky, and think about how your next breath is given by God Almighty. This is no overstatement!

Colossians 1:17 says, *"He is before all things, and in him all things hold together."* A believer has no fear, because God is the Most High. He is not intimidated or surprised by anything. In the midst of what happens to us and what we do, we have a shelter from everything. When temptations come, we have a shelter. When attack comes, we have a shelter. When disappointment comes, we have a shelter. We also have a shelter in good times.

Earlier I asked, what is the shelter of God? Psalm 91:2 tells us that God himself is our shelter. With this joyful thought, let's dwell, live, walk, and exist in a 24/7 love relationship with the Almighty, who is our shelter.

God Is My Teacher

IN JOHN 16, JESUS PREPARED HIS DISCIPLES FOR THE HORRIBLE EVENTS of the crucifixion. The disciples were filled with sorrow because of what Jesus told them. They really believed he was the promised Messiah who would deliver Israel and bring a new order to their lives. How could he be the Messiah, the God-Man, if he was to be murdered? With comforting words, Jesus told them that they would not be left orphans but that the Holy Spirit of God would come to be with them. This wonderful third person of the trinity would comfort, guide, and teach.

The Holy Spirit is the great teacher. He is the One who shows our spirits what is of God and what is not. His knowledge is perfect. His love and care for the people of God is perfect because he seeks to glorify Jesus (John 16:14).

Most of us have been in school institutions. All human beings are in the school of life, but believers have the unique honor of being in the School of the Spirit. Only one person has complete and perfect knowledge, and that is God. In fact, he is a God of Knowledges, according to the original Hebrew of 1 Samuel 2:3. This fact alone gives us confidence in what the Holy Spirit of God tells us. He is a trustworthy teacher.

He has no agenda but complete truth. Sometimes the truth of what he teaches is about our need for forgiveness. We call this conviction. At other times, he teaches us about which direction to take in life.

Yet the greatest thing he teaches us is who Jesus is! Whenever we have a revelation of the character of Jesus, it is a work of the great teacher, the Holy Spirit. Jesus becomes alive in us as we listen intently to the Holy Spirit. In fact, practicing the presence of Jesus the Holy Spirit will cause us to sense his presence with us.

The apostle Paul said that Christians should not walk in darkened understanding, because they didn't learn Christ that way (Ephesians 4:17–20). The Great Teacher reveals the greatness of Jesus. We are no longer unsure about who Jesus is. The Holy Spirit makes sure of that. As we enjoy the wonderful life God has richly given us, let's humbly learn what (and who) the Holy Spirit will show us. He is the Great Teacher!

PART FOUR:
The Ministry of God

God the Freedom Fighter

FREEDOM IS A GIFT OF JESUS, GIVEN TO US AND RECEIVED BY FAITH. Even though one might struggle with addictions, the freedom that God fights for is freedom from the bondage of trying to be good. Trying to obtain salvation through the law is what God frees us from.

One might not see this as terribly important, but God looks at it a different way. He inspired the apostle Paul to write a group of churches in the region of Galatia about the salvation that was won by the freedom fighter, Jesus Christ.

The law can do many things. It can guide us, teach us (Galatians 3:24), and tell us about God's character. It's like a mirror showing us a dirty face or a hair out of place. But the law cannot give energy to our flesh; it can give us the standard, but it cannot give us the power to please to God.

The law is a powerless negative. Don't do this, don't do that. It has no power to change us. Only faith in Jesus Christ gives us freedom.

Some have hoped that if they do enough good things, it will outweigh the bad and God will wink at them. The problem is that we couldn't possibly do enough to outweigh just one sin against a Holy God.

The good news of the gospel is that Christ has done it! He alone has done what no man can do for himself, and thus has set us free: *"So if the Son makes you free, you will be free indeed"* (John 8:36). Jesus freed us from the burden of keeping the law as a result of placing faith in who he is.

He is the one who justifies us (treats us as if we never sinned). He is the one who sanctifies us (cleans us up). He is the one who frees us from the law. Jesus has set us free to relate to God as our father with confidence and without fear. Unfettered by guilt and empowered by his Spirit, we come to him not out of duty but motivated by our love for him.

It is Jesus Christ who has made us free. We don't make ourselves free by doing good works. We could never do anything to earn salvation.

Isaiah, in shame, wrote, *"And all our righteous deeds are like a filthy garment; and all of us wither like a leaf, and our iniquities, like the wind, take us away"* (Isaiah 64:6).

If we come to God on the basis of our own law-keeping, then our law-keeping must be perfect.

No amount of obedience makes up for one act of disobedience; if you're pulled over for speeding, it won't be good to protest that you're a faithful husband, a good taxpayer, and have obeyed the speed limit many times. It's all irrelevant. You have still broken the law and are guilty. Jesus, on the other hand, is the sinless Son of God. He is the perfect High Priest.

The writer of Hebrews compared the legal requirements for the cleansing of sin:

...how much more will the blood of Christ, who through the eternal Spirit offered Himself without blemish to God, cleanse your conscience from dead works to serve the living God?

Hebrews 9:14

To accept works as a way of salvation is to minimize who God is. God is greater than our tiny attempts at cleaning up the mess we've made. The one who created a billion times a billion worlds and who holds all things together came to deal with the sin issue. The writer of Hebrews said, *"When He had made purification of sins, He sat down at the right hand of the Majesty on high"* (Hebrews 1:3).

Sitting down indicates that all is completed. We can't add anything to what has already been done by Jesus Christ. He is the freedom fighter!

God the Friend of Sinners

ONE OF THE COMPLAINTS LODGED AGAINST JESUS WAS THAT HE WAS A friend of sinners. It is rare that you find someone of great stature spending time with tax collectors and sinners, but that's what Jesus did. This irritated the religious community. One man said, *"This man receives sinners and eats with them"* (Luke 15:2). They couldn't accept that a rabbi would do such a thing. Surely the "dirty" would cause him to be dirty.

Taking the point further, it is hard to understand how God, the creator, the one who has always existed and knows all things, would lower himself to even approach mankind. Even the story of the fall of mankind in Genesis 3 reveals a God who pursues sinners.

The apostle Paul said,

> *For while we were still helpless, at the right time Christ died for the ungodly. For one will hardly die for a righteous man; though perhaps for the good man someone would dare even to die. But God demonstrates His own love toward us, in that while we were yet sinners, Christ died for us.*

Romans 5:6—8

Paul reminds us that man doesn't think like God does. He loves all. He is a friend of all, even though all have sinned. The implication is that God is full of patience and reaches out to every human being as a friend and not a judge. Oh yes, he is a judge, but first he is a friend.

God doesn't pick and choose as man does. The Pharisees couldn't believe that Jesus would lower his standards to be a friend of the worst of society. The arrogance of the Pharisees is so sad, because they, too, were sinners needing the friendship of God. They felt they were above others. They simply didn't see their own desperation. Jesus warned the Pharisees when he reminded them of their lack: *"[You] disregard justice and the love of God"* (Luke 11:42).

We can learn something from the error of the Pharisees. All of us—not just some, but all of us—are sinners (Romans 3:23), and God has chosen to reach out to us. What a wonderful reason to worship him today!

God the Light

Jesus said, *"I am the Light of the world; he who follows Me will not walk in the darkness, but will have the Light of life"* (John 8:12). When Jesus said this, he was in the temple treasury where two large lamps and many small lamps shone brightly. In wisdom, he had just dealt with the Pharisees who had tested him. In condemnation, they had brought a woman caught in the act adultery. Jesus, in perfect wisdom, as the Light of the world, rightly judged. He knew the hearts of the scribes and Pharisees. He also knew they had no interest in righteousness but in condemnation and destruction. All sin is laid bare before the Light of the world, including the sin of the scribes and Pharisees.

The Light of the world doesn't condemn but brings understanding. All of us have made choices to sin and turn our backs on the creator, but he reaches out in love. No one can hide from his blinding knowledge of our waywardness.

He also knows everything about us and is equipped to shed light on all that concerns us.

Like us, Job had many questions for God. Job lost his family, his wealth, and his health. Like all of us who experience pain and loss, Job didn't understand. In Job 38–41, God answers him with a description of who he is. God didn't defend himself by telling him that Satan had asked to test Job. Instead God shed light on who he is. It's that Job said, *"I have heard of You by the hearing of the ear, but now my eye sees You"* (Job 42:5). The Hebrew word for sees is *raah*, which means that Job understood. He had an Aha! moment. We may not understand why things happen, but the good news is that God knows. He is all-knowing, all-powerful, and all-loving. We can fully trust him when life hits us between the eyes.

In a prophecy about the coming of Jesus Christ, Isaiah wrote, *"The people who walk in darkness will see a great light"* (Isaiah 9:2). To know God, we look at Jesus.

> *And He is the radiance of His glory and the exact representation of His nature, and upholds all things by the word of His power.*
>
> Hebrews 1:3

Saul of Tarsus, who had ruthlessly targeted followers of Jesus, was on his way to Damascus one day,

> *and suddenly a light from heaven flashed around him; and he fell to the ground and heard a voice saying to him, "Saul, Saul, why are you persecuting Me?"*
> *And he said, "Who are You, Lord ?"*
> *And He said, "I am Jesus whom you are persecuting. . ."*
>
> Acts 9:3–5

Saul's name was changed to Paul and he changed into a preacher of Jesus Christ. Years later, he wrote from a Roman prison,

I count all things to be loss in view of the surpassing value of knowing Christ Jesus my Lord, for whom I have suffered the loss of all things, and count them but rubbish so that I may gain Christ.

Philippians 3:8

Paul knew that following the Light of the world was far greater than anything else. In his letter to the Colossian church, Paul wrote that God

rescued us from the domain of darkness, and transferred us to the kingdom of His beloved Son, in whom we have redemption, the forgiveness of sins.

Colossians 1:13–14

Jesus Christ dispels darkness. I don't know about you, but I want to walk in the light of his love.

God the Righteous Judge

WHEN THE APOSTLE PAUL WAS COMING TO THE END OF HIS MINISTRY
and life on earth, he summarized what had taken place:

> . . .the time of my departure has come. I have fought the good fight, I have
> finished the course, I have kept the faith; in the future there is laid up for
> me the crown of righteousness, which the Lord, the righteous Judge, will
> award to me on that day; and not only to me, but also to all who have
> loved His appearing.
>
> 2 Timothy 4:6–8

Paul then goes on to tell Timothy the sad news that Demas
had deserted him because he *"loved this present world"* (2 Timothy
4:10). Paul and everyone loving the appearing of Jesus Christ are
to be awarded the crown of righteousness by the righteous Judge
himself. Demas, on the other hand, loved the world more than the
appearing of our Lord. Sad.

I'm so glad Jesus is the righteous Judge. Since he has all the
information and is holy, he renders a fair verdict for all. He knows
those who eagerly wait for his coming and no one will be able to
disagree with his judgment.

Man cannot fool God. His perfect knowledge of us is mind-boggling. He knows our thoughts before we even have them. The greatest super-computer is a child's toy compared to God. Imagine, he can render not only a fair but perfect and knowledgeable verdict. Any man who judges another must do so with the weakness of imperfect knowledge. All mankind will witness the awesomeness of his righteous judgments.

The guilty are most often silent before a judge, especially when the verdict is given. Someday, when the righteous Judge is ready, the guilty will bow in silence, for all will understand that he is the holy, immutable, righteous judge. I often picture God's judgment day as instantaneous. God won't have to say anything. Before the righteous Judge, no one will argue their case, since all will see him in his glory and bow before his majesty. And for those feebly trying to avoid God, there will be no place to hide. His eyes will pierce the souls before him and it will be over. It will be a terrible day for some. Of special note is Paul's assurance that God was going to reward him.

There was no fear on Paul's part that he didn't measure up or that his past would catch up to him. He knew and taught Timothy that the righteous Judge knew not only how to judge but also what to judge. Paul remained faithful in his longing for his Master, the One he loved.

I can safely say that the appearing of our Lord excites me. I'm not looking out for the Antichrist or some leader of man to fix things. Jesus is who I eagerly look for. He is coming, and he is our hope. Unlike Demas, we are not to pursue the things of this world. We are to be like the deer of Psalm 42, panting for him as for a water brook.

My soul pants for You, O God. My soul thirsts for God, for the living God.

Psalm 42:1–2

It's not often that anyone wants to come before a judge, but like Paul, with other believers we have security as we look for the coming of the righteous Judge, Jesus Christ our Lord.

God the Great Savior

WITH SHOUTS OF "GOD IS GREAT," THE DECEIVED DETONATE WEAPONS that kill many unsuspecting men, women, and children. "New atheists," including Christopher Hitchens and Richard Dawkins, argue that God is not great. Still others struggle with the truth that God is great. To these, God is limited, small, unable, or vastly evil, but in him is the magnificence of goodness. God is big and he has no equal, but that shouldn't intimidate or scare anyone because God is also holy, good, and loving.

Although God is great when he heals, provides, and comforts anyone in need, the salvation he offers is the shining proof of his greatness. It is a great salvation! The writer of Hebrews reminds us that salvation should not and cannot be taken lightly: *"how will we escape if we neglect so great a salvation?"* (Hebrews 2:3)

The magnitude of his love for his creation causes him to earnestly desire the salvation of all. In fact, turning away from his free gift is against his sovereign will and makes him tiny and uncaring, if existent at all.

Two prophets who declared the greatness of God put it this way:

*Let the wicked forsake his way and the unrighteous man his thoughts;
and let him return to the Lord, and He will have compassion on him. . .*

Isaiah 55:7

Who is a God like You, who pardons iniquity. . .?

Micah 7:18

Paul chimed in by writing,

For the grace of God has appeared, bringing salvation to all men, instructing us to deny ungodliness and worldly desires and to live sensibly, righteously and godly in the present age, looking for the blessed hope and the appearing of the glory of our great God and Savior, Christ Jesus, who gave Himself for us to redeem us from every lawless deed, and to purify for Himself a people for His own possession, zealous for good deeds.

Titus 2:11–14

The difference between God and mankind is that if we were in charge, we would have blotted out humanity long ago. We are little, but the greatness of his goodness declares patience and love to all. Not only that, but God makes a way—the only way—when we couldn't do enough to be restored to relationship with him. It is the complete way. It is God's way. It's salvation through Jesus Christ!

Paul told the Ephesians,

But God, being rich in mercy, because of His great love with which He loved us, even when we were dead in our transgressions, made us alive together with Christ (by grace you have been saved), and raised us up with Him, and seated us with Him in the heavenly places in Christ Jesus, so that in the ages to come He might show the surpassing riches of His grace in kindness toward us in Christ Jesus.

Ephesians 2:4–7

God doesn't condemn with bombs. He is not evil. He sent the Son into the world *"that the world might be saved through Him"* (John 3:17).

For He [God] rescued us from the domain of darkness, and transferred us to the kingdom of His beloved Son, in whom we have redemption, the forgiveness of sins.

Colossians 1:13–14

Now that's greatness of the best kind!

Jared Anderson wrote a song of worship that I often like to sing in my private devotions. The bridge of "Amazed" expresses the worship due God: "How wide, how deep, how great is your love for me."[5]

Some distort who God is by committing terrible atrocities, and others may even deny the one who gave them life. Those who have tasted salvation direct worship to the *"GREAT KING"* (Matthew 5:35), the *"great high priest"* (Hebrews 4:14), *"the great Shepherd"* (Hebrews 13:20), and the great Savior.

---

5 Jared Anderson, "Amazed," **Where to Begin**, Integrity Music, 2004.

God the Servant King

THE WORDS "SERVANT" AND "KING" SEEM TO BE AT DIFFERENT POLES. We understand a servant to be one who has few choices and is ruled, while a king is one who rules and makes choices for all.

Consider the scene of Isaiah 6 and contrast it with John 19. Both show us Christ Jesus, although in very different circumstances. In Isaiah 6, he is the King on the throne who is worshipped. In John 19, he is the servant, dying for the sins of the world on the cross. We know Christ Jesus as a servant. The apostle Paul reminds us that Jesus *"emptied Himself, taking the form of a bond-servant, and being made in the likeness of men"* (Philippians 2:7).

This verse indicates two things. First, it shows us that he was divine in nature before becoming man. He is the King over creation itself. He rules with absolute power. Not many who make it to the top humble themselves, but that's exactly what Jesus Christ did. Do you see the greatness of who he is? He stooped very, very low.

Secondly, Jesus Christ became fully man. Some may struggle with the fact that he could be both man and God at the same time, but nonetheless this speaks to who he is. God is able to do things we cannot understand, and he does so for only one reason: love.

We can take much comfort in a benevolent King who doesn't crush others selfishly. Christ Jesus is just such a servant to mankind. Imagine: God the creator is the servant! How can this be? How can he be my servant, and yet he is. He serves us with the gift of his love.

John tells us,

> *Jesus, knowing that the Father had given all things into His hands, and that He had come forth from God and was going back to God, got up from supper, and laid aside His garments; and taking a towel, He girded Himself.*

John 13:3–4

Then Jesus washed the feet of his friends.

What motivates man to struggle to be the greatest? Is it an admission of his fallibility? God is different. Jesus knew who he was. That enabled him to humble himself. He didn't think that being equal with God was something to be used for his own benefit (Philippians 2:6).

So, what is our response to the Servant King? We can trust Jesus Christ because he has proven himself. He truly does care. The pressure is off. The only thing we need to reach for is God himself. This relieves us of all stress to attain anything. We can be people who reflect the image of Christ Jesus by serving, even though we are heirs of the great King.

As royalty, children of the King, we also love as we stoop low by his very nature that is in us. Peter put it in a wonderful way when he said,

Grace and peace be multiplied to you in the knowledge of God and of Jesus our Lord; seeing that His divine power has granted to us everything pertaining to life and godliness, through the true knowledge of Him who called us by His own glory and excellence. For by these He has granted to us His precious and magnificent promises, so that by them you may become partakers of the divine nature, having escaped the corruption that is in the world by lust

2 Peter 1:2—4

Hallelujah to God, our Servant King!

God the Builder

ALL BUILDING PROJECTS START WITH A PLAN, WHICH IS THEN FOLLOWED by tools and materials. *"In the beginning God"* opens the first chapter of the Bible. God had no tools. He had nothing to start with. Before anything was created, all that existed was God. If you're like me, your mind just can't go there, but that was exactly the case.

God didn't start with a protoplasmic blob. He started with nothing. Nothing! (Hebrews 11:3) When people are inspired to build things, they have to start with something. Only God created with nothing. Moreover, God didn't swing a hammer. He only spoke. The spoken word of God is so powerful that out of nothing came all that is. Oh, the power of God! He speaks and a billion times a billion of worlds are created.

God's plan came from who he is and not from a how-to book. By his infinite knowledge and wisdom, he created. The complexity of creation is a testament to the greatness of God.

For since the creation of the world His invisible attributes, His eternal power and divine nature, have been clearly seen, being understood through what has been made...

Romans 1:20

Man also is a builder. In Genesis 11, man wickedly planned to build for himself a city and a tower that would reach into heaven (Genesis 11:4). Did man doubt God's promise that he wouldn't flood the world again? Did man take things into his own hands, trying to protect himself? Was man so far from God that he forgot the promise and love of God? God had a plan for mankind to inhabit the whole earth. This world was built by the master builder for man to enjoy from the east to the west.

Not only did God create all things for our enjoyment (1 Timothy 6:17), he also created a way for man to have eternal life. In a state of rebellion, hopelessness, and despair, man was incapable of drafting out such a thing. God crafted the perfect plan to build a future for anyone who would only accept his love and be in relationship with him.

One of the greatest verses in the Bible is John 3:17:

For God did not send the Son into the world to judge the world, but that the world might be saved through Him.

God's plan, which he made before any of us were born, was to save us from the self-inflicted tragedy of death.

But God demonstrates His own love toward us, in that while we were yet sinners, Christ died for us.

Romans 5:8

This is the wonderful creator whom we worship: the builder of all good things! The next time you smell a fragrant flower or see beautiful colors or taste your favorite dish or hear a sweet sound, remember that the master builder provided it. Worship the creator of all—Jesus, the Christ.

God the Deliverer

THE ALMIGHTY CREATOR OF ALL BRINGS EXTRAORDINARY THINGS TO mankind. He delivers more than pizza or a registered letter. He delivers unmatched love for each and every human being that has ever lived. That may be difficult to understand, but God far transcends any comparison.

To deliver love on a global scale, he did something highly controversial. He came down to us! It would be like the postmaster general bringing mail right to someone's door himself. God didn't send an angel. This was a task too important for him to leave to anyone else. He needed to do something about our sin. So, he humbled himself by coming to us (Philippians 2:6–11). King David was recorded twice as saying, *"The Lord is my rock and my fortress and my deliverer"* (2 Samuel 22:2, Psalm 18:2). David learned that God isn't just a fire escape; he takes us by the hand and leads us out of destruction. 1 John 5:6 makes it clear that Jesus was not some gnostic phantom that was so holy that he had nothing to do with this world. The Jesus we are called to believe on is the Jesus who came by water and blood. He was a part of the real, material, flesh-and-blood world.

Not only is God approachable, he is the one who approaches us with this delivery of love. He initiates it all. And this love he brings to us ignites a response of free-will love in our hearts back to him. It doesn't make us robots but brings us into relationship.

No matter what temptations of the flesh we struggle with, Jesus came as the deliverer. His coming wasn't as a tyrant to frighten us into submission. Instead, Jesus stands at the door of our lives and knocks. He says, *"If anyone hears My voice and opens the door, I will come in to him and will dine with him, and he with Me"* (Revelation 3:20). Countless numbers of people have responded to him and become worshippers of God Almighty.

After a man was delivered from demon possession by Jesus, he couldn't help but tell others about Jesus. In fact, scripture says that the man proclaimed the *"great things Jesus had done for him"* (Mark 5:20). He was a great example of the apt response we should all give to God the Deliverer.

God the Giver

THROUGHOUT SCRIPTURE, WE FIND THAT GOD IS A GIVER. HE GIVES strength (Psalm 29:11). He gives the desires of your heart (Psalm 37:4). He gives grace and glory (Psalm 84:11). He gives what is good (Psalm 85:12). He gives perseverance and encouragement (Romans 15:5). He gives life to all things (1 Timothy 6:13). He gives us the victory through our Lord Jesus Christ (1 Corinthians 15:57). God does this and much more because of who he is.

God is a giver. He takes pleasure in giving. He is never stingy. When he gives, he overwhelms the recipient. Dozens of examples can be found in scripture, but let's focus not on what he does but on who he is. Some may be tempted to pray that God will be in a good mood and that he will grant the request made, but God is a giver. In fact, he is *the* Great Giver. When someone asks for forgiveness, God gives complete and lasting forgiveness. When someone needs healing, God gives. When someone is in need financially, God gives.

The apostle Paul told the Philippians that they should have the same attitude that Christ Jesus had (Philippians 2:5). Jesus gave himself as a sacrifice with incredible humility, the extent of which we cannot fully grasp.

Giving is not only something God does, it is something he is. Imagine how much joy God has when he forgives. In fact, we are told that there is a party in heaven every time this takes place. God specializes in giving forgiveness.

When we come to the end of our resources, he joyfully comes to our rescue. I have witnessed his amazing love as he has given in many ways. With great creativity, God has given all I have needed and more. His giving has made me very content.

God gives wisdom to those who lack wisdom (James 1:5). He does so generously and without reproach (James 1:5). John Calvin said, "This is added, lest any one should fear to come too often to God... for he is ready ever to add new blessings to former ones, without any end or limitation."[6] There is no limit to God's ability to give or to His desire to give.

Knowing that God is a giver should cause us to approach him in confidence. We can be assured that his heart is to give. Probably the most well-known verse of scripture begins by saying, *"For God so loved the world, that He gave..."* (John 3:16).

The apostle Paul told the Ephesians that he prayed God would give them *"a spirit of wisdom and of revelation in the knowledge of Him"* (Ephesians 1:17). What could be greater? To know God the Giver is the greatest gift anyone could receive.

---

6 John Calvin, "Calvin's Commentaries, Vol. 45: Catholic Epistles," *Sacred Texts*, March 13, 2014 (http://www.sacred-texts.com/chr/calvin/cc45/cc45019. htm). Translated by John King.

God the Good Shepherd

TWO SPECIFIC PASSAGES OF SCRIPTURE ARE WIDELY KNOWN BY MANY people.

> *For God so loved the world, that He gave His only begotten Son, that whoever believes in Him shall not perish, but have eternal life.*
>
> John 3:16

Children are taught early to memorize this wonderful truth.

Psalm 23 is also very popular. It paints a beautiful picture of a God who cares completely and of his sheep completely at peace. David describes God's care as providing nourishment, guidance, protection, and the abundance that comes when confidence is placed in him. We hang on to this scripture as our own personal statements of faith through the good and bad of life.

To take the theme to a more intimate level, we turn to John 10, where Jesus said that the Good Shepherd is none other than himself. We can put a name to the shepherd of Psalm 23—he is Jesus Christ, the creator of all. The one who carefully formed you and me, the one who thinks about us, the one who gave himself to purchase our salvation, is the wonderful Good Shepherd.

We could easily be tempted into dwelling on the great things the Good Shepherd does, but let's, for a moment, just think about his person.

Sandwiched between scripture about His deity is the passage found in John 10:1–18. Jesus isn't just a good shepherd as opposed to a slothful incompetent shepherd. He is God. He is the ultimate Shepherd. He has no rival. If we can trust and have confidence in anyone, it is Jesus Christ. Can we even trust ourselves? We don't have the knowledge, wisdom, and love to match God's. He is the one we can safely run to and cling to.

When challenged by life, we can draw closer to the Good Shepherd. Even better, we can remain close to him all the time. By keeping near him, we not only are safe, but we keep ourselves from wandering into lonely and dangerous terrain.

The thing that overwhelms me about God the Good Shepherd is that he is with me. As his lamb, I have the assurance of his unending presence. Like Paul the apostle, you and I can joyously proclaim that nothing can *"separate us from the love of God, which is in Christ Jesus our Lord"* (Romans 8:39). This Lord is the Good Shepherd.

God the Miracle Worker

THE CREATOR OF ALL THINGS IS CERTAINLY ABLE TO PERFORM MIRACLES. His strength and power isn't limited by anything. His love is greater than all things. Absolutely nothing is too difficult for Jesus Christ. Nothing intimidates him.

Countless testimonies can be given of what God has done, but let's focus on the miracle worker himself.

A leper needed a miracle. He wasn't only sick in his body, he was dead spiritually. The miracle he needed was more than healing, and he recognized that Jesus was the one who could perform it. He said, *"Lord, if You are willing, You can make me clean"* (Matthew 8:2). What a wonderful statement of faith. Jesus touched the leper. Oh, the great love of God that would touch! Leprosy was no match for the touch of God. No problem is too great for the touch of God.

The only challenge for Jesus was the statement of the leper, who challenged the undeniable love of God: "Lord, I believe you can perform a miracle. I just don't know if you want to." God is not only able, he *wants* to perform miracles in our lives. The character of God speaks for itself. Is God willing to perform a miracle for you or me? Yes, yes, and yes! The only limitation on God is our lack of faith in him. In fact, scripture tells us that the only time Jesus was stopped from bringing change was when unbelief was in the hearts of the people. Referring to Nazareth, Matthew wrote, *"He [Jesus] did not do many miracles there because of their unbelief"* (Matthew 13:58).

Jesus Christ is a miracle worker. That will never change, so we can go to him in faith and trust his heart. Some may say, "I haven't seen the miracle." This only reveals the fact that they are looking in the wrong direction. Remember, it's not the miracle but the one who creates miracles that we wait on. His wonderful knowledge of our situation is enough for us to rest in his sovereignty. We can say, "Lord, I know you are willing," and then trust him implicitly.

God the Source

MY WIFE AND I ENJOY HIKING. ONE DAY, WE WENT HIKING WITH friends near a mountain stream. We reveled in the beautiful waterfalls the steam had cut out of the rock. The water was so clear that I couldn't resist kneeling down and taking a drink. You guessed it. It was fresh and cool as it ran all the way down the mountain to a river. It was the source of nurturing water for the animal life round about it.

God Almighty is the source of all things. He started it all. From his lofty position above all things, he spoke and created a billion times a billion worlds. Then, as the source, he formed man with his own hands.

Just who is this One who has no beginning and end? He is the creator. He is the source of life. He is more than that: he is the source of all that is needed for life.

Salvation isn't even possible from anyone or anything other than the source of all life. He is the one who initiates all. The apostle Paul wrote,

> . . .*He has now reconciled you in His fleshly body through death, in order to present you before Him holy and blameless and beyond reproach. . .*
>
> Colossians 1:22

Paul goes on to say that *"in Him you have been made complete, and He is the head over all rule and authority"* (Colossians 2:10). Jesus Christ is the source of eternal life.

He is also the source of healing, since he knows every cell of our bodies. No matter what your theology may be, let's consider the source of health and healing: God Almighty. God is mightier than all sickness. God knows every detail of our lives, including things unknown to us or anyone else. He is the source. Not only does he know everything about us, he is able to fix us, since life comes from him. He is the source.

Along with salvation and healing, he is the source of real life. Apart from him, there is no real life. His love for us is so great and so complete that life is full of joy, contentment, and satisfaction. That's why, as believers, we can face life's challenges with the calm assurance that troubles will pass without destroying us. I have known people who enjoy life this way. What can intimidate a child of God?

> *Who will separate us from the love of Christ? Will tribulation, or distress, or persecution, or famine, or nakedness, or peril, or sword?*
>
> Romans 8:35

Paul goes on to say, *"But in all these things we overwhelmingly conquer through Him who loved us"* (Romans 8:37).

The worship of God is reasonable, because he is the wonderful and glorious source.

Conclusion

ALMIGHTY GOD IS SO MUCH MORE THAN WHAT HAS BEEN OUTLINED IN these pages. What we do know about him is what we're able understand through the lens of our lives. Jesus is the light of the world, but he's more than a metaphor of light. Like people, God is unique. He enjoys. He can be grieved. He can be engaged personally. He's not an impersonal robot but is complex, beautiful beyond anything man has experienced, and will be our joy to know for all eternity. Of course, if anyone decides to live independent of the creator, they'll receive their wish, but why would anyone make such a choice?

God makes the invitation for eternal fellowship to all of humanity. If you've read this book but cannot say that you know God personally, I invite you to pray this prayer:

> *God, I confess that I am a sinner. Forgive me and make me new. Walk with me and talk with me. Help me to live for you. Surround me with people who will point me back to you. Thank you for saving me and giving me new life. Help me to share what you've done for me and in me.*

If you prayed that prayer and meant it, I can say with certainty that you will know and experience the creator in ways you cannot imagine. If you don't have a Bible, get one and begin to mine the rich jewels that are found in it. Begin with the Gospel of John. Finally, find others who also know the creator. You'll be amazed at what you learn about him, and then you will naturally tell others about him as your life reflects the discovery who he is.